SIGNS OF ENCOURAGEMENT

100 SIGNS FOR YOUR JOURNEY OF FAITH

Set up road signs; put up guideposts.
Take note of the highway, the road that you take.

Jeremiah 31:21 NIV

LISA DONELSON

Copyright © 2020 by Lisa Donelson

ISBN: 978-1-7352570-3-7

Deluxe Color Edition

Signs of Encouragement: 100 Signs for Your Journey of Faith
Published by Speak Life, 745 31st Ave E, West Fargo, ND 58078

Donelson, Lisa, 1962-
Signs of Encouragement : 100 Signs For Your Journey of Faith / Lisa Donelson.
ISBN: 978-1-7352570-3-7
1. Religion – Christian Living – Devotional. 2. Religion – Christian Living – Spiritual Growth. I. Title
242

Scripture quotations marked (NLT) are taken from the Holy Bible, New Living Translation, copyright ©1996, 2004, 2015 by Tyndale House Foundation. Used by permission of Tyndale House Publishers, a Division of Tyndale House Ministries, Carol Stream, Illinois 60188. All rights reserved.

Scripture quotations marked (TLB) are taken from The Living Bible copyright © 1971. Used by permission of Tyndale House Publishers, a Division of Tyndale House Ministries, Carol Stream, Illinois 60188. All rights reserved.

Scriptures quotations marked TM are taken from the THE MESSAGE: THE BIBLE IN CONTEMPORARY ENGLISH, copyright©1993, 1994, 1995, 1996, 2000, 2001, 2002. Used by permission of NavPress Publishing Group

Scripture quotations marked (NKJV) are taken from the New King James Version®. Copyright © 1982 by Thomas Nelson. Used by permission. All rights reserved.

Scripture quotations marked (NIV) are taken from the Holy Bible, New International Version®, NIV®. Copyright © 1973, 1978, 1984, 2011 by Biblica, Inc.™ Used by permission of Zondervan. All rights reserved worldwide. www.zondervan.com The "NIV" and "New International Version" are trademarks registered in the United States Patent and Trademark Office by Biblica, Inc.™

Scripture quotations marked (AMPCE) are taken from the Amplified Bible, Copyright © 1954, 1958, 1962, 1964, 1965, 1987 by The Lockman Foundation. Used by permission.

Scripture quotations marked (Phillips) are taken from the J. B. Phillips, "The New Testament in Modern English", 1962 edition, published by HarperCollins.

All rights reserved. No part of this book may be reproduced or transmitted in any form or by any means, electronic or mechanical, including photocopying and recording, or by any information storage and retrieval system, without permission in writing from the publisher.

DEDICATION

*This book is dedicated to Jesus, my Lord and Savior.
The one who gave me the ideas for the sign messages.*

To my husband, Tom, for his unconditional love and support.

*And to the Christian Writer's Group in Fargo, ND.
You always cheer me on. Without your encouragement, this book would not have been published.*

CONTENTS

Introduction	8
Faith	11
Love	23
Life	35
Prayer	47
Trouble	59
Salvation	71
The Cross	83
Thanksgiving	95
Christmas	107
New Year / New Beginning	119

INTRODUCTION

When asked about the signs, I always said, "Everyone has a relationship with Jesus, they either love Him, hate Him, or are ignoring Him." I wonder, what kind of relationship do you have? No matter what you think of Jesus, Jesus loves you!

The short sayings at the beginning of each reading appeared on roadside signs along Highway 2 in northeastern Minnesota for almost seventeen years. The messages were meant to encourage those who love Jesus, and make everyone else think about their relationship to God. They were bright pink letters on big black signs. Maybe you traveled that road and saw them.

I believe the roadside signs were, *Signs of Encouragement*, for people traveling the highway. My husband Tom and I owned the property next to Highway 2 just east of Floodwood, MN. We had purchased the signs hoping to rent them. The business never developed. Instead we put a message of encouragement on the signs in our yard. We put a different message on each side and changed them each month. We knew people would read whatever they saw beside the road. I saved most of those sayings in a computer file. This book is a collection of some of those sayings, along with a short devotional reading.

Over the years, many kind people stopped to visit with us because of the signs. We have received notes in our mailbox and met many great people who love Jesus. Some of the people we count as friends to this day. One man, early on in the sign ministry, was going through a very bad time in his life. He loved Jesus, but his life was kind of a mess. He was on his way to Duluth one day, and as he went past our place, he noticed the signs. He said to himself, "If those people are in the yard when I come back from Duluth, I am going to stop." Tom was over at the neighbors having coffee that afternoon. He had a strong feeling he should go home. Just as he drove in the driveway, this man was coming past on his way home. He saw Tom in the driveway and turned around to stop. He and Tom visited that day and Tom encouraged him. We are still friends with him and we have seen God do amazing things in his life.

Another time, a lady stopped to say thank you for putting up the signs. She told me she had driven to work every day past our signs and was always encouraged by the message. She was retiring from her job and just wanted to let us know how much she appreciated the signs.

Others stopped to take pictures. Some stopped to tell us the message on the signs was just what they needed. Sometimes they told us the message had encouraged conversation with others they were riding with who did not know Jesus.

Many have asked where the messages come from. Often, I just had a feeling about a particular topic. So while driving, or early in the morning when I woke up, or sitting in church, I would start working with an idea and God would help me develop it into a message to fit on the signs. You know, it could only be so many letters across, it could only be four lines long. The message had to fit on the sign. Also, when driving by at 60 miles an hour, a person can't read a long message.

I know God used the black signs with the pink letters to bless many over the years. They have blessed us also. Many times the message spoke to our hearts and lives as well as those going past on the highway.

May the abundant blessings of a life lived with Jesus be yours. May you know His peace which passes understanding, the love of the one true God, and the fellowship of the Holy Spirit, both now and forever.

AMEN.

FAITH

Now faith means putting our full confidence in the things we hope for, it means being certain of things we cannot see.

Hebrews 11:1 Phillips

1

GOD WILL OPEN DOORS WHEN NO ONE ELSE CAN

Let me share a testimony about our God who opens doors. One of my friends found out she had fast-growing breast cancer. She needed surgery and many chemo and radiation treatments. She and her husband did not have health insurance, or the finances to pay the bills themselves. However they DID know how to pray! God helped them find a grant that would pay up to a million dollars in expenses for her treatment. The grant was not based on income. What a blessing! God opened a door for them!

Prayer and praise are the two things that will open the doors of heaven. One of the best things we can do for our family and friends is to pray for them. We know every spiritual battle is fought in heaven, as well as by those of us on earth. What a blessing to know we serve the Mighty Warrior himself, Jesus, who will open doors when no one else can. Whatever challenges you are facing today, talk it over with Jesus and let him show you what to do. He wants to be your burden bearer and your champion.

For everyone who keeps on asking receives;
and he who keeps on seeking finds;
and to him who keeps on knocking, [the door] will be opened.
Matthew 7:8 AMPC

2

WHEN YOU FOLLOW JESUS YOU ARE NEVER LOST

When we walk by faith, it is important to follow the path God has planned for us. It is much easier to follow God and walk in His way than it is to try to make our own way through life without a path to follow. God does not promise us a wide and easy way. In fact, Jesus says in Matthew 7:13-14 the pathway to heaven is narrow and few find it.

It says in God's word in Ephesians chapter 1, He chose us before the foundations of the world were laid. God has good plans for us as His children. He has things only YOU can do. If you are going to do the things God has prepared for you to do, then you have to follow His path for your life. This takes faith. Sometimes it is hard to see the path, and sometimes, honestly, we get off the path and have to find our way back. We serve a faithful God who tenderly leads us when we allow Him to.

Take some time this week to consider the path you are on right now. Is it the path God has set out for you? Are you spending time reading your Bible and seeking God's plan for you this week? Do you need to make any course corrections to get back on the right path? Have you lost the path entirely? If so, ask God to help you. He is faithful and will show you how to find the path again. Trust in His ability to lead you. He loves you and desires the best for you at all times.

For I have stayed on God's paths;
I have followed his ways and not turned aside.
Job 23:11 NLT

3
HIS EYE IS ON THE SPARROW
HE SEES YOUR NEED TOO

When we had the black signs with the roadside faith messages in our yard, people would occasionally stop to comment on the sign, or tell us a story. When the message above was on the signs, a woman stopped one day and talked with my husband. She commented on how the song, *His Eye Is on the Sparrow* was one of her Mom's favorites. She told him her mom had recently passed away. She said what a blessing the sign was to her, as a reminder of how God was watching over her during her time of grief.

God always knows our needs. Each day, as you begin your day, ask Jesus to help you with whatever you are facing. From the smallest detail to the biggest problems, He knows your needs and He wants to help. He is a loving and compassionate God who SEES you. Just like he sees each sparrow and pays attention to everything that happens. Never forget, He's on your side, He's there for you, even when you don't feel it. Trust Him. He knows your need before you ask. You will not be disappointed when you have faith in God.

But not a single sparrow can fall to the ground
without your Father knowing it.
Matthew 10:29 NLT

4
GOT QUESTIONS JESUS HAS THE ANSWERS

How often must God wonder about our indecision when His word clearly speaks to us? There are times when we can't decide if we should choose path A or path B when following God. He is faithful when we put our trust in Him. We ask ourselves, "Is this my idea? Or God's idea?" It seems so unclear sometimes, but I believe God created us with the ability to choose. We are not just robots doing the same thing all the time. I think it delights Him to see what we will choose at times. He is a creative God, not a God who demands we do things one way. He gives us room to explore and find our way as we follow Him. He does have a right way, and there are rules to live by, but we also have some choices within those guidelines.

God can work with us, even if we chose the path that may take longer to get to the destination He has planned for us. When we ask God, and spend time seriously listening for answers, we will get them. Sometimes the answer is *not yet* and sometimes it is *no*, for a reason we cannot yet understand. And sometimes it is YES! Those are the answers I like the most! But no matter what the answer is, we know we can trust Jesus to always give us the RIGHT answer!

You said, 'Listen and I will speak! I have some questions for you, and you must answer them'
Job 42:4 NLT

5

STOP DOING THINGS YOUR WAY YIELD TO GOD'S WAY

Are you the type of person who always has to have your way? Some people call it stubborn, others call it strong-willed! I know I sometimes struggle with this. My ancestry is German, so I can be very strong-willed! But of course, it is not all in my genetic makeup. A lot of my stubbornness has to do with not being willing to yield my will, either to God, or sometimes to others.

One challenge I faced was with sharing a car. For most of my life, since I was sixteen, I have had my own vehicle. I could go where I wanted and do what I wanted within reason. Several years ago, one of our vehicles was in an accident, and my husband and I decided, rather than replace it, we could share a vehicle. We live in town, so it seemed reasonable at the time. I discovered though, it is a constant source of frustration for me to not have a vehicle available when I want it. It really does not matter so much if my husband picks me up late from work if I have nowhere else important to be. Or, if I get the groceries today or tomorrow. It is all about what I want to do. My frustration comes from my stubborn will and my unwillingness to yield to another plan. This area of yielding my desires to God and others is one I am still working to get right! Pray for me! The more I walk by faith and trust God to be in control of my life, the less I have to do things my own way.

Are you willing to yield to God when He asks you?

But the wisdom that is from above is first pure, then peaceable, gentle, willing to yield, full of mercy and good fruits, without partiality and without hypocrisy.
James 3:17 NKJV

6

DRINK LIVING WATER
NO FILTER NEEDED

In the book *Glory Days* by Max Lucado he used the example of cutting an apple in half, putting half of it in a bowl of clear water and the other half in a bowl of battery acid. After thirty minutes which half would you want to eat? Our minds are like that apple. If we soak them in all the negative things which happen around us, it is like acid eating at our mind and our soul. If we soak them in God and His word, it is like fresh water. Drinking living water is even better. When we drink the living water of God's word, we will never be thirsty again. And unlike most of our water supply today, it does not need to be filtered!

Jesus is not talking about natural thirst when he says we won't be thirsty, but rather the kind of spiritual thirst that leaves us always wanting more. The living water God provides us through His word is pure and holy. When we have faith in God and His Word, we are drinking living water. As you mature in your life with Jesus, you will find you have less thirst for the things which are common in this world and more thirst for the heavenly life to come.

Jesus replied, "If you only knew the gift God has for you and who you are speaking to, you would ask me, and I would give you living water."
John 4:10 NLT

7
FEED YOUR FAITH AND YOUR DOUBTS WILL STARVE

Do you have areas in your life that are challenging for you? Have you ever tried to focus on renewing your mind in these areas to think about them the way Jesus would? We all seem to have particular parts of our lives the Holy Spirit works on in us, to change our thinking from the natural, world's way of thinking, to God's way of thinking. The world tells us *seeing is believing* but God tells us *believing is seeing.* We need to believe what God says in His Word is true, then we will see it with our eyes.

Feeding our faith, means we are reading God's word daily and listening to music which honors God. We are reading books and articles which help us grow in our faith. The best way to remove doubt from your mind about anything you are concerned about is to seek God with your whole heart. I had a friend who liked to apply the *worry test.* She would say, "If you are trusting, you are not worrying, and if you are worrying, you are NOT trusting!"

If you want to starve out the doubt and worry in your life - don't feed it!

Yes, be bold and strong! Banish fear and doubt! For remember, the Lord your God is with you wherever you go.
Joshua 1:9 TLB

8

GOD IS ALWAYS GOOD
GOD IS ALWAYS FAITHFUL

Are you a faithful friend? Friendship is a lot of work! It takes time and effort to maintain a friendship. When my mother, who was born in 1922 was young, her only friends were those from school and church. If a friend moved away, the only way to keep in touch was with a hand-written letter. No email, no texting, no phone call even!

In the world we live in, it is much easier to stay in touch with our friends. But do you? Sometimes I think all of those things that are supposed to save time, just take more of it. I'm sure my mother did not have over thirty close friends. If she would have had a Facebook account, it would have looked like she did not know anyone! But maybe less is better when it comes to really close friends!

God is a friend who is ALWAYS there for you. You can call out to Him at any time and know He hears you. He wants to develop a friendship with you where you talk and He listens, but He also wants times with you where you LISTEN and He talks! If you have not tried it lately, then quiet your mind for at least five minutes and allow the Holy Spirit to speak to you in ways you may not expect. He loves you more than you can ever understand and He will always be a faithful friend.

The Lord is a friend to those who fear him,
He teaches them his covenant.
Psalm 25:14 NLT

9

IT'S NOT WHAT YOU BELIEVE THAT MATTERS; IT'S WHAT YOU OBEY

Obedience is not one of those words we like to hear. Especially when we need to apply it to our own life. We don't like to take our thoughts captive, or our eating habits, or even our poor attitude at times.

Do you believe Jesus died for you? If your answer is yes, then your life should reflect it. You may wonder how it is possible. One way is in our attitude toward others. The Bible says Jesus had compassion for everyone He met. He tells us if someone asks for our cloak, we should give him our shirt too. (Luke 6:9) Give more than what is asked of you, go out of your way to be gracious and kind to others, especially to those who are not very likable.

When we obey the instructions in the Bible, we are reflecting the love of Jesus and His way of doing things. It is true, we are not saved from hell by our actions, but our actions show we belong to Jesus and prove He is our Lord and Savior. Being saved by grace is how we get to heaven when we die. Our faith shines through our actions.

But someone will say [to you then], You [say you] have faith, and I have [good] works. Now you show me your [alleged] faith apart from any [good] works [if you can], and I by [good] works [of obedience] will show you my faith.
James 2:18 AMPC

10

OUR GOD IS FAITHFUL
HE WILL MEET YOUR NEED

Have you ever made a list of your needs at the beginning of the year? This is a great way to see how God is at work in your life. If you make a list, you can pray over those needs daily and see how God meets them. Don't get discouraged though, if some of your needs keep moving to the list for the following year!

Our God IS faithful. He is ALWAYS faithful to those who are faithful to Him. He wants to see our lives filled with good things that give glory to Him and His kingdom. Remember the words from the Lord's Prayer: *Your Kingdom come, your will be done, on earth as it is in heaven.* (Matthew 6:10 NIV)

If you are in the middle of a crisis today, ask God to show you what you should do. You can even ask Him how to pray and expect His Holy Spirit to guide you in your prayers. Be careful, don't mistake wanting your own way for God not answering your prayers. He always knows what is best for us, even when we don't know ourselves. Trust Him to meet your needs in the best way for you. Have faith in God to guide you.

Understand, therefore, that the Lord your God is the faithful God who for a thousand generations keeps his promises and constantly loves those who love him and who obey his commands.
Deuteronomy 7:9 TLB

LOVE

Dear children, let's not merely say that we love each other; let us show the truth by our actions.

I John 3:18 NLT

11

REAL LOVE TAKES ACTION

Let the love of Jesus flow through you today! "How do I do that?" you might ask. Well, you put love in action. It can be a simple thing, like being kind to someone in line with you at the store. Or maybe even the cashier, who sees so many people they become a blur. A kind word and a smile can make their day. Or it can be something more, like fixing a meal for someone who is lonely or tired or sick.

My Mom was a sweet Christian lady and a great example. Toward the end of her life she was not very mobile, but every few weeks we would go shopping together. She didn't drive, so I would take her wherever she wanted to go. One week she needed some fabric at a fabric store. I parked right beside the door in the handicapped spot, she said, "You just go in and get what I need." I agreed. When I came out of the store, she was sitting in the car smiling at the people who came out of the store, through the car window. I asked her what she was doing. "Giving out smiles", she said! She was showing the love of Jesus in the best way she knew how, just by smiling at people and letting the love of Jesus flow through her.

When we allow the love of Jesus to flow through us to others, we DO love. Will you find a way to DO love with me today?

Since God chose you to be the holy people he loves, you must clothe yourselves with tenderhearted mercy, kindness, humility, gentleness, and patience.
Colossians 3:12 NLT

12

THE LOVE OF GOD IS BIGGER THAN ANY PROBLEM YOU FACE

If you have giant problems in your life, you need to know God is bigger than any *giant* you face. When King David was a young boy, he faced the giant Goliath. Do you think David heard the story about the Hebrew spies and how only Joshua and Caleb had the courage to fight the enemy? (Numbers 13:25-33) Maybe as he faced the giant Goliath, he was thinking about how he was going to be strong and courageous just like Joshua. (I Samuel 17:32-49)

Be strong and courageous today as you face the giants in your life, knowing God is on your side. God loves you, He will fight for you. He is able to bring you through the battle. God will never leave you or forsake you. Your problems are His problems when you are His child. As you develop your relationship with God, you will understand more and more how much He loves you. Thanking Him for His care for you and for His help, will give you confidence in His ability to help you overcome any problem you face.

The Holy Spirit is the part of God living in us. God sent Him to be with us after Jesus rose from the dead. He will always stand with you, no matter what you are up against.

I shall ask the Father to give you someone else to stand by you, to be with you always. I mean the Spirit of truth.
John 14:16-17 Phillips

13

PERFECT LOVE CASTS OUT FEAR
GOD'S LOVE IS PERFECT

In church one Sunday, during worship time, I was thinking about how much God loves us. His love is powerful and complete. When I don't trust Him with absolutely everything, it's as if I don't think He loves me very much.

If I really had a better *heart knowledge* of how much God loves me, I would not be concerned at all about any of the difficult things in my life. I would simply trust Him to guide me and take care of me. It is one of the areas I am still working on.

Isn't it wonderful God always gives us a little something to work on? Something which will deepen our relationship with Him, no matter where we are in our Christian walk. Allowing love to overcome fear in our lives is one of the things many of us work on. The enemy likes to make us afraid and tell us all the things we can't do, and all the things that won't happen. When you hear a negative voice in your head, most of the time it is the enemy and not God. God wants you to trust Him to guide your steps. He wants you to rest in His love for you. When you are afraid, just whisper, "Jesus I love you". Let His love overcome your fears.

We know how much God loves us, and we have put our trust in his love. God is love, and all who live in love live in God, and God lives in them.
I John 4:16 NLT

14

GOD KNOWS ALL ABOUT YOU AND HE STILL LOVES YOU

Do you enjoy shopping at garage sales? Or do you like a good thrift sale? I am a thrift store shopper. Not because of the recycling thing, mostly because I can't see spending so much money on items that are available for much less in perfectly good condition. I have also found a few 'one of a kind' items at the Thrift Store. For me, it's all about finding the treasure. God has always been in the business of seeking out the lost one, the hurting one, the one who does not know Him. He wants us to seek Him too.

Some thrift stores are called *second chance* stores. God is all about second chances, and third and fourth, etc. Isn't it just wonderful our God is always there for us? No matter how often we try to take the wrong road, He is always there calling us back to a life lived close to Him. He knows all about you. He loves you, it does not matter what is in your past. Let Him give you another chance.

Maybe you needed to know this today. He holds you close. He wants to guide your every step! He loves YOU!

See, I have tattooed your name upon my palm.
Isaiah 49:16 TLB

15

THE WORLD SAYS, GET ALL YOU CAN JESUS SAYS GIVE ALL YOU CAN

Why does summer always go so fast and winter drag on? Every day has the same amount of hours in it. We really don't have a lot more winter months than summer ones in the north! I hope you make time to enjoy both summer and winter activities with your family and friends. Time with family and friends is SO important. The world is always pulling us in different directions. It is good to put down your phone and have a conversation with your family, your friends, and with God.

Nothing on this earth is more important to God than relationships with the people He has placed in our lives. Spending time with people is one of the best ways we can give to others. Jesus wants us to give of our time and our talents, as much as He wants us to give our financial resources. If you are struggling today with balancing work, your activities, and spending time with family and friends, I would encourage you to re-evaluate how you spend your time. Ask God to show you what HE wants you to do, and then be willing to let go of those activities that are not on *His* list!

Teach us to number our days and recognize how few they are; help us to spend them as we should.
Psalm 90:12 TLB

16

LOVE IS MORE THAN A FEELING
LOVE IS A CHOICE

We see a lot of hearts and candy during February, the month we celebrate Valentine's Day. Everywhere you look there are hearts representing love. If you truly love someone, you will be committed to them. You will *choose* to love them, even when they are not very loveable.

We hear a lot about love, and devotion. Romantic love is everywhere in February. The world says if you really love your sweetheart you should get them a big box of candy, right? But maybe candy is not the best thing for them. It may not even be the thing that makes them feel the most loved. Each of us has different things that speak love to us.

God loves us deeply. He cares about us, and He wants us to live a life pleasing to Him. A life that reflects His love for us, to others. God always speaks our love language. He knows us intimately and chooses to love us, even with all of our flaws.

Trust in the perfect love of God, even if you don't know what He is doing. The love relationship between you and God is not based on feelings, it's based on a choice. A choice you make, and one God made thousands of years ago. Every day, choose to love God and choose to love those He has put in your family.

Let your unfailing love surround us, Lord,
for our hope is in you alone.
Psalm 33:22 NLT

17

NO MATTER HOW BAD YOU MESS UP GOD STILL LOVES YOU

I know there are times in my life, and some of them recently, when I have said too much. I get started down a path and then even though I hear the small voice inside my head, (or my heart) saying, "you should probably turn back," (or stop talking), I just don't. I end up either feeling bad I said so much and can't take it back, or having to apologize. But I can't take it back, no matter what.

It is good to remember words spoken cannot be unspoken. This is particularly true with those closest to us. When we are tired or upset about something, it is often best to remain silent if possible or say as little as possible. It's a little like getting a haircut, once it is cut off, it can't be put back on. Use your words wisely. When you are upset, stop and pray before you speak. Remember God always loves you, even when you mess up. If you do end up saying the wrong thing, ask for forgiveness, first from God, then from the person you hurt. Then be sure to forgive yourself too. God will keep on loving us. We need to accept His love.

Too much talk leads to sin. Be sensible and keep your mouth shut.
Proverbs 10:19 NLT

18

LOVE IS A FOUR LETTER WORD USE IT OFTEN

Usually when we mention *four-letter words* we are talking about swear words most of us don't use! But LOVE is also a four-letter word. One you can use often! But consider what you apply it to. Remember the Bible says, God is love (I John 4:8). His nature is to love everyone. Everything He is, is wrapped up in unconditional love. So if we say things like, "I love that shade of pink", is it the best use of the word love which is another name for God? Maybe not. You can think it over and come to your own conclusion.

How often do you tell your people how much you love them? When you say "I love you" to your spouse, or your child, or your parent, please think about how much they mean to you, and how much God loves them as well. I am not sure we can ever fully understand the depth of God's love for us, His children. His love is wider than the ocean, which we can't see across and deeper than the deepest valley. Spend some time today considering how much God loves you, and asking Him to reveal His love to you in new ways.

I hope your day is full of the love and joy only Jesus can give!

Your unfailing love, O Lord, is as vast as the heavens;
your faithfulness reaches beyond the clouds.
Psalm 36:5 NLT

19

THERE IS NO LOVE LIKE THE LOVE OF JESUS

Did you know Jesus cares about EVERYTHING that happens in our life? We all have big things AND small things every day which causes us concern or frustrates us. Some things give us joy and others' sorrow. God cares about all of them. You may have concerns about how to pay next month's rent, or how to deal with an illness you or someone in your family is facing. You may be considering a major decision, like where your next job will be, or what house to buy. Or your concerns may be smaller like what to wear to work today, or what your kids are doing today. Or even what to make for supper!

Our wonderful Savior loves us so much He cares about EVERY decision we make. He cares most about people. And He cares about the condition of your heart. He is a wonderful, loving Father God who always cares about the things that matter to each of us. Never forget it.

...Look at the lilies of the field and how they grow. They don't work or make their clothing... And if God cares so wonderfully for wildflowers that are here today and thrown into the fire tomorrow, he will certainly care for you.
Matthew 6:28-30 NLT

20

DO SOMETHING DIFFERENT WRITE GOD A LOVE LETTER

In my personal study, I have been focusing on the love of God. Since God IS love personified, we can always have a deeper revelation of how much He loves us. One little quote I have on a sticky note on my computer is *A heart full of love produces a face full of joy*. There are days I need to work at loving, and days it comes easily.

One way to increase our understanding of how much God loves us is to read His word. The letters written by John in the New Testament (I, II, III John) are a good place to start. A father always recognizes his children. He loves them in a way no one else can. They belong to him and he will fiercely protect his children. God is like that with us, He will protect us and provide for us even better than any earthly father.

You could try writing your own *love letter* to Jesus. Tell Him how much you love Him. How thankful you are for what He has done for you by saving you from the penalty of your sin. When you are done writing, imagine Jesus sitting next to you. Read your letter to Him, let Him know how much you love Him! He loves to hear from His children, just as a loving earthly father enjoys hearing how much his children love him.

See how very much our Father loves us, for he calls us his children, and that is what we are! But the people who belong to this world don't recognize that we are God's children because they don't know him.
I John 3:1 NLT

LIFE

The thief comes only in order to steal and kill and destroy. I came that they may have and enjoy life, and have it in abundance (to the full, till it overflows).

John 10:10 AMPC

21

LIFE'S MESSY LET GOD CLEAN IT UP

Do you ever wake up in the night with all the stuff of life going through your mind? Often when it happens, it is difficult to go back to sleep. Or maybe something else wakes you up in the night. One night I woke up with pain in my stomach, for no apparent reason. So, I said to myself, "I am not going to lie here and worry about the pain", instead I prayed. I thought, I know lots of people who need prayer, so instead of focusing on my pain, I'll focus on praying for others. The pain went away and didn't come back.

My Mom would often wake up in the night and find it hard to get back to sleep. Her solution was to sing hymns to herself and pray. The same could apply to praise songs and prayer. You may not go right back to sleep, but it is better to focus your mind on praise and prayer than the cares of the world.

Life can get very messy at times. My Dad used to say, "It will all come out in the wash if you add enough soap." Including God in the cleanup process is where the soap comes in. God knows how to clean up any mess you encounter in life. When your life gets messy, let God clean it up. He is a master at clean up.

Have mercy upon me, O God, According to Your lovingkindness; According to the multitude of Your tender mercies, Blot out my transgressions. Wash me thoroughly from my iniquity, And cleanse me from my sin.
Psalm 51:1-2 NKJV

22

LIFE GOT YOU DOWN
LET JESUS LIFT YOU UP

Wouldn't our world be a boring place if we only had sunshine, or we only had rain? Isn't God good to send us both? Just like our lives, we have good days, and not so good days, but the not so good ones make us appreciate those great days all the more. How would we know the difference if everything was always the same?

Whatever you are facing today, get your strength from the Lord. The Bible says, *Be strong in the Lord and in his mighty power* (Ephesians 6:10 NIV) If we get discouraged and want to give up, then we let the enemy win, resist the enemy, and hold on to Jesus who always gives us the victory!

The best way to let Jesus lift you up when you are struggling, is to just say a short prayer, "Jesus, help me through this." Name the thing you need help with and believe He hears you and wants to help you. Praise Him for the help that is on its way. Thank Him for hearing you and helping you. Jesus set the example for us when He was here on earth.

But you belong to God, my dear children. You have already won a victory over those people, because the Spirit who lives in you is greater than the spirit who lives in the world.
I John 4:4 NLT

23

GOD CAN MEET ALL YOUR NEEDS LET HIM

Have you ever felt kind of down, or even truly depressed? Maybe sometimes you feel like you need to get your joy back? I have sometimes felt that way. It is like a cloudy day, you know the sun is shining, just not where you are!

I want to remind you though, we have a *faithful* God. He is always there, even when you don't feel His presence, you can count on Him. When we pour out our hearts to Him in prayer, He hears us, and He is with us and will comfort us. This comfort will help us to get the *Joy of the Lord* back in our hearts. It will help you enjoy living again.

I know we all have something in our lives which is a major concern; family, health, finances, etc. This is a part of our life on earth. You can be assured God hears your prayers, and will meet your needs. Most of the time when we are in need we tend to look around. We ask, how can we solve this? God wants us to let HIM meet our needs. So instead of looking around, look UP to God. Even if it takes a while for the answer to come, don't give up. He is always faithful to His promises. Praise Him and experience the power praise brings, even when you feel down.

Yet he (Abraham) refused to allow any distrust of a definite pronouncement of God to make him waver. He drew strength from his faith, and while giving the glory to God, remained absolutely convinced that God was able to implement his own promise.
Romans 4: 20-21 Phillips

24

PEACE IS THE GIFT OF GOD
FEAR IS THE TOOL OF THE DEVIL

Uff Dah! (Norwegian for good grief, loosely translated!) What a busy day today in my office! Have you had days like that? You have your day planned, and then a bunch of unexpected things pop up disturbing your plans. Unexpected things can pop up suddenly in life as well. But do you let them disturb your peace too?

Did you know fear and peace are direct opposites? The devil always wants you to be afraid. Afraid for your family, your financial situation, your health, everything you do. But God does not want you to live in fear. He wants you to trust Him with everything and live in peace with those around you. Fear also steals our joy in life. It says in John 10:10 the thief comes to *steal, kill and destroy*. One of the names of Jesus is Prince of Peace. Peace belongs to those who have Jesus in their hearts. Don't allow feat to rule your life.

If we keep our focus on Jesus and let Him guide us through the ups and downs of the day, we will come to the end of the day with peace in our hearts and minds. Another verse I like is, *You will keep in perfect peace all who trust in you, all whose thoughts are fixed on you!* Isaiah 26:3 NKJV. Fix your thoughts on Jesus today and allow His perfect peace to push away your fear.

The Spirit however, produces in human life fruits such as these: love, joy, peace, patience, kindness, generosity...
Galatians 5:22 Phillips

25

WE KNEEL FOR THE CROSS AND STAND FOR THE FLAG

The 4th of July was one of my Dad's favorite holidays. I think it was some combination of love for his country (Dad was a WW II veteran), a paid holiday in the middle of summer, and watermelon. We absolutely could not celebrate the 4th without watermelon, and some fireworks of course! I have very good memories of the 4th of July with my family! It was a day of being together and having fun. We always stayed home, had a good meal, and enjoyed each other's company.

As Christians, it is important that we honor our flag, it stands for the hard-won independence we have in the United States. It is even more important for us to honor the cross. It symbolizes freedom from death and the grave. Our bodies die and are buried, but our spirits pass from this life on earth to our life with Jesus in heaven. When we asked Jesus to be our Savior, he gave us power over death. Death no longer has a hold on us. We do not need to fear it. I have heard many stories of Christians dying, it is always a peaceful passing. They are not afraid, they see their Savior, Jesus, with open arms, waiting for them.

I hope you and your family honor the cross and the flag every day. Even though things do not always look very good in our country, God is still with us. Jesus will be our shelter in every storm of life.

Then if my people who are called by my name will humble themselves and pray and seek my face and turn from their wicked ways, I will hear from heaven and will forgive their sins and restore their land.
I Chronicles 7:14 NLT

26

ON THE ELEVATOR OF LIFE ARE YOU GOING UP OR DOWN

How important are your feelings? Have you ever felt mad at God, or sad about how things are working out for you? Do you sometimes feel like you are on the tenth floor and other times feel like you are in the basement?

Do you question why your prayers are not answered the way you want? I think we have all been down that road at one time or another. Certainly we see it in the lives of the prophets. God is big enough, He can handle anything we throw at Him. Consider the story of Job in the Old Testament. During his lifetime he experienced great success, total destruction, and then complete restoration. God's mercy and grace were there for him and they are always there for you.

Sometimes I think the only thing that makes God really sad is when we turn away altogether. I have thought in the past, I can at times control what I know and how I think, but it is much harder to control how I feel. I do my best though, not to base my faith on how I feel, but rather on what I KNOW about God. At the end of my life, I want to be going UP, not DOWN! I know God is UP! Keep looking UP my friends!

For the Lord God is our sun and our shield. He gives us grace and glory. The Lord will withhold no good thing from those who do what is right.
Psalm 84:11 NLT

27

MAKE GOD'S DAY BE OBEDIENT TO HIM

Do you ever feel like you spend a significant amount of your life waiting? Waiting at a traffic light, waiting in line at the store. Sometimes we have to wait on God for answers. I think God waits for us to hear and obey. We can use those times of waiting to pray and ask God what He wants us to do.

Have you ever had this situation come up with your spouse? We will be planning on doing something together. I will say to him, "Are you ready? I'm waiting for you." And he will say, "Oh, I was waiting for you!" It makes us both smile.

It seems the important thing with God is to try to keep the communication line open so we can hear from Him. Have your daily prayer time, and read the Bible regularly to understand God's way of doing things. When you are quick to do whatever He asks of you, He will give you more assignments. God loves it when we are obedient to His still small voice. What is He asking you to do today? When we participate daily in God's plan for us, we can expect more assignments!

Does the Lord delight in burnt offerings and sacrifices as much as in obeying the Lord? To obey is better than sacrifice, and to heed is better than the fat of rams.
I Samuel 15:22 NIV

28

BIBLICAL MATH
GOD MULTIPLIES, SATAN DIVIDES

This is a catchy saying, but it is also true. God always multiplies what we give Him to work with. Consider the story of the loaves and fishes. The story is told more than once in the Bible about Jesus feeding a multitude of people with a few small loaves of bread and a few fish. (See Matthew chapters 14 and 15) In both stories there are leftovers besides! More leftovers than what they started with. That has never happened at my house! But God does multiply what we give Him.

Satan divides. He comes to steal and kill and destroy the Bible says in John 10:10. He divides families and friends, husbands, and wives. His purpose is ultimately to divide us from Jesus himself. To make us question if God loves us and is working all things for our good. If you find yourself questioning God's love for you, it is most likely the whispering voice of the enemy asking those questions, just like in the Garden of Eden - "Did God REALLY say?" (Genesis 3:1) Don't let Satan divide you from Jesus and win the battle for your soul.

Then he told the people to sit down on the grass. Jesus took the five loaves and two fish, looked up toward heaven, and blessed them. Then, breaking the loaves into pieces, he gave the bread to the disciples, who distributed it to the people. They all ate as much as they wanted, and afterward, the disciples picked up twelve baskets of leftovers.
About 5,000 men were fed that day,
in addition to all the women and children!
Matthew 14:19-21 NLT

29

BE A LIFE BULB
LET YOUR LIGHT SHINE FOR JESUS

Let the love of Jesus shine through me, is often one of my prayers. We are blessed to live in a time when it is very easy to turn on the lights. We flip a switch, and we have light. Most of us don't even give it much thought, myself included. When Jesus was on earth, the lights were not as bright. There were no street lights or flashlights. The only light in a home came from a burning wick in a dish of oil. Some more fortunate ones had what we would recognize as an oil lamp. Still, Jesus says He is the *light of the world* (John 8:12). When you shine the light, no matter how dim, you chase away the darkness. The love of Jesus is light and hope to a world full of dark shadows.

It amazes me at times how Jesus positions the right people, in the right places, at the right time, to light our way. If you need help today, I pray the Lord will send someone with His light into your life. Or, maybe you are a helper, one God can use to light the way for others. Then pray He brings you those you can help the most. God is always actively involved in our lives. What a blessing. Let your internal light shine out so others can see the light of Jesus in you!

No one takes a lamp and puts it in a cupboard or under a bucket, but on a lamp-stand, so that those who come in can see the light.
Luke 11:33 Phillips

30

LEAVE THE PAST BEHIND FOCUS ON A FUTURE WITH JESUS

What is in your past? Do you have good memories of your growing up years, or not? My husband did not come from an ideal home, but then most of us did not have a perfect life growing up. Even if you were blessed to have a home with a mom and a dad, brothers and sisters and friends, and a stable environment, still, I'm sure there are some memories it would be better to forget!

I once received a birthday card that said, *Life doesn't have to be perfect to be wonderful.* I agree with the statement completely! In many ways, my life is not perfect. My husband and I were never able to have children, our financial situation was often paycheck to paycheck, but in the middle of all of it, I can say with certainty, I am BLESSED!

I can say it because my life is centered on Jesus and He makes it wonderful. Focusing on Jesus and His mercy and grace allows me to leave the past behind and focus on my future with Him. Knowing God is well able to do exceedingly, abundantly, above ALL I can ask or think (Ephesians 3:20) gives me hope for the future.

My brothers, I do not consider myself to have fully grasped it even now. But I do concentrate on this: I leave the past behind and with hands outstretched to whatever lies ahead I go straight for the goal— my reward the honor of being called by God in Christ.
Philippians 3:13-14 Phillips

PRAYER

The earnest prayer of a righteous person has great power and produces wonderful results.

James 5:16b NLT

31

THERE IS POWER IN PRAYER ARE YOU PLUGGED IN

Have you ever had a great prayer meeting in the car on your way to work, just you and God? If not, you should try it one day! Start with a praise song or two, you can even try to make up the words yourself if you are in the car alone! Then just share your heart with God. He always wants to hear from you!

In my personal life, I am always expecting great miracles. I believe in living a life of expectancy. Many of you may be in a place where you are ready to see a miracle from God in one area of your life or another. When you plug into God, wonderful things happen in your life. A lamp only gives off light when it is plugged in. We too must plug-in to Jesus for His light to shine through us.

The areas in our lives where we need the most power from God are usually family relationships, money, and health. If you are at a point where you need to receive a miracle, I encourage you to keep believing. Never give up, stay plugged-in to God's power. Trust God's timing in your life. All praise and thanksgiving to our All-Wise, Wonderful, Creator God!

He does great things too marvelous to understand.
He performs countless miracles.
Job 5:9 NLT

32

PRAYER IS THE BRIDGE BETWEEN PANIC AND PEACE

Let me share with you what God has put on my heart recently. I was reading in Hebrews Chapter 4. I love the last verse about coming boldly to the throne of grace, but I also love those mysterious verses about rest. God has prepared a place of rest for His people.

Do you ever wish life had a *pause* button, just like the TV? I think God would like us to use the pause button a bit more than we do each day. Have you ever noticed how He is generally not in a hurry? So often in life, things take a lot longer than we wish. We hurry from one thing to the next always trying to get more done in a day than we possibly can.

I would encourage you to learn to hit the pause button in your life every day for even just 15 minutes to spend time resting in God's presence. He loves it when you just sit quietly with Him and listen to His voice and read His Word, the Bible. He will show you things you have never seen before. When you pray, you cross over from panic to peace. When trouble comes into your life, your first response is generally to panic about what to do. God calls us to pray instead and rest in His peace.

So let us come boldly to the throne of our gracious God.
There we will receive his mercy, and we will find grace
to help us when we need it most.
Hebrews 4:16 NLT

33

KEEP ON PRAYING
DELAY IS NOT DENIAL

We often think just because we are not seeing any answers to our prayers, God is not going to answer us. And we often give up. I once heard a Pastor say God was less about *microwave* than He was about *slow roasting*. In other words, we want everything yesterday, but God has His reasons for taking His time. One reason is to teach us to rely completely on Him.

When I look back, I am so thankful for God's patience. I know it is better to wait a bit for God's perfect timing than to have what I wanted when I wanted it.

I also try to remember what I want to see happen in my life is not all about me! So often, God is at work on a much larger picture than what I can see. I am a part of the plan, but only a part. I have to wait for the other pieces to be in place before my piece will fit into the puzzle. When you work on a picture puzzle, you can't put a middle piece in until you have the pieces around it. You can't tell exactly how it fits.

Today, if you find yourself frustrated by waiting for the just-right time for the *just-right answer*, don't give up. Keep on praying, delay is NOT denial!

O Lord, come back to us! How long will you delay?
Take pity on your servants!
Psalm 90:13 NLT

34

GOD IS CLOSER THAN YOUR CEL PHONE AND HE CAN ALWAYS HEAR YOU

I went out to lunch recently with a good friend. We went to a local restaurant where they have free pie with any order, one day a week. They had the best Peach Supreme pie! What a treat! It is really good to enjoy the little things in life. Especially when you have *big things* you are waiting for. Each of us has a particular prayer concern. It may be a family issue, a job situation, health, or finances, or some other area of your life. I would encourage you to look for the ways God is at work in your life EACH day.

Pray about your concerns. God is always listening when you pray. You don't need to reach for your phone, He is always available to hear your prayer. His signal never drops, and it never has static. He hears every word, spoken from your mouth, or your heart.

Here is my prayer for you today:

Lord Jesus, make yourself real to my brothers and sisters in Christ in a new way today. Show them your great love. Let their rejoicing know no limit as they celebrate the great things you are doing in their lives and the lives of those around them. Let your healing, restoration, and power be evident in their lives so they will have great testimonies to share with family and friends of what a wonderful God they serve. Amen.

For the Lord your God is the God of gods and Lord of lords.
He is the great God, the mighty and awesome God,
who shows no partiality and cannot be bribed.
Deuteronomy 10:17 NLT

35

THE POWER OF PRAYER IS MIGHTY FOR EVERY NEED

How do we know God hears us when we pray? Do you find yourself praying the same things over and over and then wondering if God will ever answer your prayer?

I know God has answered many prayers. Sometimes, it seems like we wait a long time for an answer. And sometimes we don't get the answer we expect. Here is a short testimony about quickly answered prayer.

One winter, my husband was working part-time plowing snow. The first few times he went out, he had a partner to work with who was not a nice guy. One Saturday night snow was in the forecast, so we prayed, either it wouldn't snow enough to plow, or God would intervene and allow someone else to work with him. It did snow, but when he got to work the usual guy was out of town, so he had a different partner. The new partner was a much nicer guy. God answered our prayer.

It is a simple thing, and some may say it would have worked out that way even if we hadn't prayed. I believe, before we called, He answered (Isaiah 65:24). I believe nothing happens by chance. God sees everything and He, and the angles, are actively involved in our lives every day.

Prayer is a mighty tool, handle it with care.

You can throw the whole weight of your anxieties upon him,
for you are his personal concern.
I Peter 5:7 Phillips

36

PREVAILING PRAYER MEANS YOU NEVER GIVE UP

Have you ever quit praying for something because you did not get the answer you expected? At times we pray over a particular concern for a few weeks, or maybe even a few months, but when nothing seems to change, we just give up. It somehow seems easier to give up, than to keep on praying.

When I get to the place where I feel like my prayers are not being answered, I remember a man I knew at one time whose wife was not a believer. For more than thirty years he prayed for her daily, and every Sunday he attended church alone and then spent the day fasting, all the while believing she would one day ask Jesus to be her Savior. Before she died, she gave her life to Jesus. His prayers and persistence won the battle. He showed me what it means to prevail in prayer.

If in your heart, you know what you are praying for is in line with God's will for your life, then don't give up! Keep on praying. Tomorrow might be the day your prayer is answered. Keep on believing and hoping, even when it is hard.

Base your happiness on your hope in Christ. When trials come endure them patiently, steadfastly maintain the habit of prayer.
Romans 12:12 Phillips

37

GOD DOESN'T USE VOICEMAIL HE ANSWERS EACH CALL

How easy it is for us in our technology-centered world to ignore someone. I am guilty of this. In my office, I am not particularly fond of sales calls. I know people need to make their living this way, and companies depend on the calls to generate business. But, I don't always like answering them, so I let them go to voicemail!

God doesn't do things that way. He does not pick and choose which calls He will answer today. He does not have someone screening His calls. He has the ability only God can have to hear each person when they call, no matter how many calls are coming in at the same time! Now that is multitasking at its finest!

He loves all His children so much He always pays attention when they call to Him. Never think God is too busy to hear your prayer or pay attention to your concerns. When you are calling out to God, you will never get put on hold, or have your call go to voicemail!

The Lord hears his people when they call to him for help.
He rescues them from all their troubles.
Psalm 34:17 NLT

38

TIME SPENT IN PRAYER IS NEVER WASTED

One spring my husband and I took a trip on a train. We were on a very tight schedule to make a connecting commuter train when we arrived, and then to get a rental car before the rental agency closed. So, we started praying that God would help us to make the connections. We asked our friends to pray for us as well.

The mainline train did end up being delayed by about fifteen minutes. We had a window of about forty-five minutes to get on one of three commuter trains if we were going to get our rental car before the agency closed. If we got on the first one, we had plenty of time, the second one, just enough time, the third one, well, not really enough time. With the main train being fifteen minutes late, we were pressed for time to get to the second commuter train. Added to the problem was not knowing our way around the train station, and the commuter train station was in another building over a block away. As we got to the area to board the commuter train, the one we needed was boarding. There was no time to buy tickets at the window. We knew the tickets would be more expensive on the train, but we needed to be on that train! So we got on. When the conductor came through to collect the tickets, we were ready to pay the upcharge, but the man beside us gave the conductor his punch card and told him to just take our fare off of his card. What a blessing! And we arrived at the rental car agency on time too.

God answers prayer, sometimes in very unexpected ways!

I am praying to you because I know you will answer, O God.
Bend down and listen as I pray.
Psalm 17:6 NLT

39

PRAYING TOGETHER IS THE MOST POWERFUL THING ON EARTH

Do you have a prayer partner? Someone you can go to when you need someone to pray with you? If you are married, it may be your spouse, but it may not. You may have several prayer partners. If you are fortunate, you know a prayer warrior, someone who seems to have a direct line to heaven! Often these people are mature in their faith. They have been believers for many years and have seen answers to prayer on many occasions. They may have also experienced times when God has said "no", or "wait" and they have learned when to change course, or when to just be patient.

If you and your spouse pray together, you are indeed blessed. Having a prayer partner to agree with you in prayer over your children, your household, your finances, your career, and your daily needs is a wonderful blessing. My husband and I have had the habit of praying together daily for many years now. We have seen God answer our prayers, and we have had times when we had to be persistent in prayer as well.

Nothing is more powerful than praying together. Agreeing with someone in prayer over their health, or any other concern they might have, helps them to connect with God, the one in control of the universe. Find someone to pray with today!

And I tell you once more that if two of you on earth agree in asking for anything it will be granted to you by my Heavenly Father.
For wherever two or three people come together in my name,
I am there, right among you!
Matthew 18:20 Phillips

40

START YOUR DAY THE JESUS WAY PRAY

The best way to begin each day is by spending time reading God's word and praying. As you do this, be on the lookout for God appointments each day. You may discover opportunities to share a word of encouragement with someone. God often puts us in the right place at the right time. Sometimes He wants us to pray with someone about their need. It could be on the phone, at work, at the lake, in your backyard, in the store or a restaurant, anywhere you happen to be, any day of the week.

What a blessing we can share our love for Jesus with those who cross our path. Each day, as you ask God what assignment He has for you today, be open to the leading of the Holy Spirit within you and see what amazing things God will do through you!

You can pray this simple prayer each morning, "God, I'm available today for whatever you need me to do." You may be amazed at the opportunities that come your way! Be sure to share those experiences with other believes too, so they can be encouraged!

For I know the plans I have for you," says the Lord.
Jeremiah 29:11a NLT

TROUBLE

*In my desperation I prayed, and the Lord listened;
he saved me from all my troubles.*

Psalm 34:6 NLT

41

NOTHING JUST HAPPENS GOD IS ALWAYS IN CONTROL

In the book of Exodus, God sent Moses to tell the Israelites He was going to deliver them, but before they got delivered, things got worse. (Exodus chapters 3-7) It wasn't as if God was not at work, rather He wanted to show Himself mighty. God had a plan to deliver them with great power and might, so everyone, including the Egyptians would know He was God. It may have looked to the Israelites as if God was not helping them, but they could not see the end of the story. Many times, we cannot see how our current circumstances are working for our good. We have to believe God is in control of everything that happens to us. It says in the Bible, God directs our steps. I never want Him to stop.

Sometimes I think things get worse in my own life before they get better. It's like when I clean my closet. I have to make a mess before it looks better. It is important to keep in the forefront of our mind that God is at work, even if we can't see how it will work out for our good. In the end, everything will turn out for our good, because He does all things well.

And we know [with great confidence] that God [who is deeply concerned about us] causes all things to work together [as a plan] for good for those who love God, to those who are called according to His plan and purpose.
Romans 8:28 AMPC

42

HEMMED IN ON ALL SIDES LOOK UP TO JESUS

I know everyone faces challenges, in our families and our daily lives. My prayer for you today is when you feel hemmed in by life, you will turn your gaze upward, rather than looking around. Jesus is always up. Looking up, means we are looking at Him. Not only to meet our needs, which He wants to do, but also for comfort and courage to face whatever comes.

I once heard a famous speaker say when we reach the bottom of the pit, there is only one way to look, and that's up. Jesus is always looking down, ready to give us a hand up.

When we face trials, it is so important to keep our thoughts focused on Jesus and what He would have us do for His Kingdom. We need to focus on the things we ARE able to do, not on what we are NOT able to do! Even when we are still in need, we can generally find someone else who needs an encouraging word or a friendly smile. Who is He prompting you to help today? Being other focused is a real help when we are in the midst of our own personal storm.

After saying all these things, Jesus looked up to heaven and said,
"Father, the hour has come.
Glorify your Son so he can give glory back to you."
John 17:1 NLT

43

WHEN THE GOING GETS TOUGH CHRISTIANS LEAN ON JESUS

"Are you ready for winter?" This is a common question to ask as the daylight decreases in the north. Are any of us ever ready for anything coming our way? Or for a new season in our lives? Change takes place regularly as we live our life. Babies are born, loved ones go home to heaven, we move from one location to another, or change jobs.

One way to always be ready for anything is to trust Jesus to help us and take care of us. Toward the end of my Mom's life, she had some physical challenges. She told me she was able to get through them with courage and grace because she knew Jesus was helping her. She said she wished more people understood how much Jesus would help if they only asked. He knows the path before us, and He knows our past as well. He goes before us, and behind us and surrounds us with His peace and love. We can always rest in Him and trust Him. Remember to lean on Jesus when life gets hard.

Do not be anxious about anything, but in every situation, by prayer and petition, with thanksgiving, present your requests to God.
And the peace of God, which transcends all understanding, will guard your hearts and minds in Christ Jesus.
Philippians 4:6-7 NIV

44

STOP WORRYING START WORSHIPING JESUS

Have you ever noticed *worry* and *worship* both start with w-o-r? Too bad I can't think of a great acronym to use with W-O-R! Jesus talked about worrying. He said it never added a single moment to our day, and He was right, of course! (Matthew 6:27) So why do we so often worry about things we have no control over? We worry about the weather, our hair, our children, our spouse, our job. None of our worrying ever accomplishes anything except to make us upset.

Next time you find yourself worrying about something, try worshipping Jesus instead. Find a favorite verse and memorize it. Repeat it over and over when you are tempted to worry. Something like Psalm 23:1. *The Lord is my Shepherd, I shall not want*, or as the NIV translation puts it, *The Lord is my shepherd, I lack nothing*. There is an old chorus based on the Living Bible version, it starts, *Because the Lord is my shepherd, I have everything that I need.*

You can also worship Jesus by singing songs of praise to Him. If you work in an office, you may not want to sing out loud, but you can always hum quietly, or sing in your mind. The important thing is to turn your thoughts from your worries to worshiping Jesus. He knows your needs before you ask and He wants you to trust Him with everything.

The Lord is my shepherd; I have all that I need.
Psalm 23:1 NLT

45

GOT PROBLEMS NO ONE UNDERSTANDS LIKE JESUS

One day during my prayer time, I thought about how the struggles in our lives often require us to hang on to our faith, similar to a tug of war with a rope. If we ease up, then we lose ground, we have to keep pulling, even if we don't feel like we are winning. The problems in our lives can make us feel like we are in a tug of war. Sometimes we are gaining ground, and sometimes we are losing it.

The big difference in a Christian's life is this, Jesus has His hands over ours on the rope, He lends us His strength when we feel like we have no more strength left to pull. He does not even wait for us to get tired, He is just always there, helping us. No matter what we are going through, no one understands how to help us better than Jesus.

We also have limited vision. We never know what is ahead for us. We may feel like we are wearing a blindfold in our tug of war. We wish we could see if we are winning, but we can't. Jesus can see what is ahead for us and He is always on our side.

So if you feel like you are in a tug of war today, and you are wearing a blindfold, and cannot see the progress, just keep pulling. Trust Jesus to see your progress and help you pull!

He gives power to the weak and strength to the powerless.
Isaiah 40:29 NLT

46

WHEN THE STORMS OF LIFE COME CLING TO JESUS THE ROCK

What do you do when the storms of life come your way? Do you hide under the covers and just hope it will all blow over, or do you set your face into the wind and keep pushing on?

I suppose you want to know what I would do, well, sometimes one thing and sometimes the other! Sometimes I have the energy and strength to fight the battle. At other times all I really want to do is go to bed! I know at those times the enemy of my soul is winning the battle, but I also know Satan will NOT win the war!

Many people struggle with depression. It can be very debilitating, to the point of not being able to keep a job or do things normal people do. My husband suffered from clinical depression for a time. It was a hard time for both of us. I remember a time when the only thing I knew to pray was, "God help my husband". The depression did not lift in a few days, or even a few months, but eventually, it gave way, and things changed for the better.

We all face storms in our life. But we serve a *faithful* God, who has promised *never* to leave us or forsake us. (Hebrews 13:5) So even when the storms of life come your way, hold fast to Jesus, he will be your anchor in the storm. If you don't have the energy to fight the battle, then go to bed with a prayer in your heart, "Jesus, help me". And He will.

He lifted me out of the slimy pit, out of the mud and mire;
he set my feet on a rock and gave me a firm place to stand.
Psalm 40:2 NIV

47

GIVE GOD GLORY NOT GRUMBLING

It is always so amazing to me when I read the Bible how little human nature has changed. Our world is entirely different, but humans are really not much different today than we were thousands of years ago. We still struggle with the same issues and we still overcome them by the power of the Holy Spirit within us.

One day, I was considering the part of Exodus that tells the story of how God's people were set free from their captivity, and then they started complaining. (Exodus chapter 16) I thought, *it is really hard for God to bless a complainer.* How often do we find ourselves complaining about our situation? We complain about the weather, or about our work, or the people we work with. Instead of complaining, we should learn to pray, and then praise God for the blessings He has given us. I made a new commitment that day to praise more and complain less!

If you are looking for some help with how to praise God, the Psalms are a great resource. Find a few and mark your favorites! Memorize a few verses for those times you are tempted to grumble, and give God glory instead of grumbling.

Give unto the Lord, O you mighty ones,
Give unto the Lord glory and strength.
Psalm 29:1 NKJV

48

TOUGH TIMES TEACH TRUST
TRUST GOD, HE KNOWS YOUR NEED

Several years ago I led a women's Bible study which covered all 66 books of the Bible. It was called *The Amazing Collection.* Some of the scriptures made me think, like Habakkuk and his questions to God. "God, what are you doing?" And, "What is happening?" And God's answer, "If I told you, you wouldn't even understand", my loose translation. (See Habakkuk chapter 1)

Sometimes in life, when we follow Jesus, we end up going where we didn't want to go, but He is always with us. He cares for us, even when we don't understand what He is doing. It is then our trust and faith can grow stronger if we lean hard on Jesus.

If you find yourself facing tough times right now, my prayer for you is to lean into Jesus and allow Him to do whatever work He chooses in your life. Let the tough times teach you how to trust Him more. Instead of allowing difficulties to make you angry or bitter, let God use them to make you a better person.

For the revelation awaits an appointed time;
it speaks of the end and will not prove false.
Though it linger, wait for it; it will certainly come and will not delay.
Habakkuk 2:3 NIV

49

WHEN TROUBLE COMES THE JOY OF THE LORD OVERCOMES

Have you ever faced serious trouble in your life? The kind where you have no idea how you are going to get through this situation? One strategy I use, especially when driving, is to turn up the praise music! It not only lifts my spirits, but it also covers up any of those unusual noises my vehicle may be making! The enemy hates it when he is doing his best to push us down and we just won't stay down! Remember those little toys called Webbles? They had rounded bottoms. The tagline was *Webbles wobble, but they don't fall down!* Determine to be a Webble, don't let Satan keep you down!

Remember, we serve a MIGHTY GOD who is able to do EXCEEDINGLY, ABUNDANTLY, ABOVE ALL we ask or think according to His word. (Ephesians 3:20) Hold on to our Mighty God for whatever your need. Let the joy He puts in your heart overcome your concerns about the problem. He will help you. Your circumstances are not a surprise to God. He is able to work miracles in your life. Don't look at your situation from the world's view, instead ask God to show you how HE sees it, and go with His perspective.

As they began to sing and praise, the Lord set ambushes against the men of Ammon and Moab and Mount Seir who were invading Judah, and they were defeated.
2 Chronicles 20:22 NIV
(Read the whole story in 2 Chronicles 20!)

50

LIFE IS HARD
HEAVEN IS ETERNAL

We all walk through hard times in life when we really can't understand what God is doing. Times when God asks us to hold on to hope, even in what seems to be a hopeless situation. The challenges of life give us opportunities to stretch our faith. Opportunities to ask God for bigger things than we have asked for before. The opportunity to lean in, rather than lean away.

When you find yourself in the middle of a particularly difficult challenge it is good to keep your focus on the eternal rather than the temporary. Our lives here on earth are certainly temporary. If we have eighty years, or ninety, it is still a limited life span. Heaven is not limited. Heaven is an eternal dwelling place. A place prepared for us by our Savior and friend, Jesus himself. He told his disciples He was going to prepare a place for them. He has prepared a place for you too. (John 14:2)

I want to encourage you today. I want to assure you Jesus wants to lead you, no matter what your circumstances. He IS working something good through you, in you, and for your future. The good may even be for someone else you meet along the way. Jesus uses everything in your life for good. Hold on, heaven is on the horizon.

So we do not look at what we can see right now, the troubles all around us, but we look forward to the joys in heaven which we have not yet seen. The troubles will soon be over, but the joys to come will last forever.
2 Corinthians 4:18 TLB

SALVATION

*Jesus answered, "I am the way and the truth and the life.
No one comes to the Father except through me."*

John 14:6 NIV

51

DO YOU KNOW JESUS TELL SOMEONE ABOUT HIM

Take a few minutes today to think about your friends. Friends are like flowers along our path of life. We gather them as we move from one area to another, or from one job to another. My experience has shown me there are friends for a time and then there are friends for life. Never underestimate your influence on BOTH types of friends or their influence on you.

Pray for them, especially when God brings them to your mind. The Holy Spirit is very good at prompting us to pray, if we stay in tune with Him. Even if you have not seen someone for a long time, if you think of them, pray for them. And when you have an opportunity, tell them about what God is doing in your life, then ask them what He is doing in their life! If they don't know Jesus as their Savior, be sure to share the good news of the Gospel with them.

I always feel blessed by the friends God puts in my life. Both the ones who are friends only for a season and the ones who stay friends for life. Friendships built around the love of Jesus are the brightest flowers in the garden of life!

Friends come and friends go,
but a true friend sticks by you like family.
Proverbs 18:24 MSG

52

IF YOU BELIEVE JESUS DIED FOR YOU GIVE HIM CONTROL OF YOUR LIFE

One Saturday morning, during some private prayer time, God gave me a very clear mental image. He does that sometimes with me. If I quiet my mind and heart and seek Him, He will at times give me a mental image that speaks to me.

This one was an image of me driving a car. I had both of my hands white-knuckled on the steering wheel. God said to me, "Lisa, I WILL NOT peel your hands off the wheel." He meant me to understand I was the one who had to let go and allow Him to steer. He would not force me to give him the steering wheel to my life. I had to be willing to let go and let Him take over.

When we ask Jesus to be our Savior, we are also inviting Him to have control of our life. To be open to His leading and prompting. To learn to know Him and His way of doing things and to be willing to adapt to His ways. This can take the form of learning to clean up our language, or what we read, or the music we listen to.

Take a few moments this week to examine your life. Are there any areas where you have not been willing to allow Jesus to have His way? Are there areas you need to *take your hands off* so He can guide you? He loves you so much. You can trust Him. He died for YOU!

That means you must not give sin a vote in the way you conduct your lives. Don't give it the time of day. Don't even run little errands that are connected with that old way of life. Throw yourselves wholeheartedly and full-time—remember, you've been raised from the dead!—
into God's way of doing things.
Romans 6:12-13 MSG

53

IF YOU LET HIM
JESUS WILL WHITE OUT YOUR SIN

Most of us will admit we have lied at one time or another. Small white lies or outright total deception. The best way to deal with any of it is to confess it to God and allow His grace to wipe away our sin.

Do any of you remember the old style White-Out sold in a bottle with a brush like fingernail polish? It would often dry up and cake, and sometimes it was really hard to spread it on just right without leaving smears or lumps! Now we have "tape" white-out. It rolls on and covers up the error. If you have really sharp fingernails, you might be able to carefully scrape it off. Not true when Jesus applies the *white out* to your sin. When He puts it on, it covers completely and can never be removed. When you confess your sin to Him, He erases it. It is gone for good, never to come back again as far as He is concerned.

Stay close to Jesus this week by being honest with Him about every part of your life. He already knows, but He wants you to be forgiven. You can only experience forgiveness when you confess your sins. Let Jesus take away your sins and give you a new beginning.

"Come now, let's settle this," says the Lord. "Though your sins are like scarlet, I will make them as white as snow."
Isaiah 1:18a NLT

54
IF YOU DON'T HAVE JESUS WHO DO YOU HAVE

We all put our hope and our trust in something or someone. Some of us trust our parents, or our family or friends. Some of us only trust ourselves. We believe no one is more trustworthy than ourselves. Living that way can be a lonely life.

Family and friends can fail you when you least expect it. I have experienced it in my own life. I have found the only one I can fully trust is Jesus. I trust my husband, he is a good man, but he cannot always be with me. I would like to say I trust myself, but I know I do not always make the best choices. When I ask Jesus to help me, He is always willing to guide my decisions. I get into the most trouble when I don't ask for help.

So, back to our question. If you don't have Jesus, who do you have? Who or maybe what, is your God? And how is that working for you?

Looking back on your life, can you remember times when you trusted Jesus to guide or direct you? What about times when you didn't? When you put your faith in Jesus, the Son of the Living God, you are in good hands. He is all-knowing, all-wise, and He knows the beginning from the end. He truly has a *big picture view*. Put your trust in Him today and relax, He's got this!

I will satisfy him with a full life and give him my salvation.
Psalm 91:16 TLB

55

DRIVE SAFELY
ESPECIALLY IF YOU DON'T KNOW JESUS

This road sign saying was one of my favorites! I had it on the signs one year in May, over Memorial Day weekend. We had A LOT of traffic past our house on Highway 2 in northern Minnesota on holidays. This roadside sign saying was a bit tongue in cheek. We did want EVERYONE to drive safely on the highway, no matter what type of relationship they have with Jesus. But there is a certain contentment in knowing when the time comes for our life to end here on earth, our eternal destination is assured. It is if you have asked Jesus to be the Lord of your life, the Savior of your soul!

If you don't know Jesus, perhaps today is a good day to ask Him to be your Savior. Pray this simple prayer, "Jesus, forgive my sins, cleanse me and make me whole. I give you my life and I make you my Lord and Savior." When you turn your life over to Him, you can be sure He will watch over you all the way to your eternal home, no matter how or when that transition happens.

So when you are out and about on the highway, or just traveling along the road of life, drive safely. And introduce your family and friends to Jesus, so you will be sure to see them again in heaven.

It is good both to hope and wait quietly for the salvation of the Lord.
Lamentations 3:26 TLB

56

WHERE WILL YOU SPEND ETERNITY SMOKING OR NON-SMOKING

A long time ago this saying was on a bumper sticker. Although this is a catchy saying, it is a serious question. There is a very big difference between heaven and hell. There are also a lot of people who believe there is a God, but they don't necessarily believe in heaven and hell as real places. If you believe a part of the Bible, you should believe ALL of it.

If you read the Bible, you know there is certainly a difference in where you spend eternity. Eternity is a VERY long time. Jesus tells us about heaven and hell. He tells a story about a person who wanted out of hell, but it was not going to happen. He had made his choice while he was on earth (Luke 16:19-31).

We all must choose our eternal residence while we are here on earth. When you believe in your heart and confess with your mouth that Jesus Christ is the son of God and has the power to forgive your sins, you are on your way to an eternity in heaven. (Romans 10:9-10)

I'll take non-smoking, what about you?

Don't be afraid of those who can kill only your bodies—
but can't touch your souls!
Fear only God who can destroy both soul and body in hell.
Matthew 10:28 TLB

57

A LIFE WITHOUT JESUS IS LIKE THE SKY WITHOUT THE SUN

I do not know many people who do not like a sunny day! Cloudy days just seem more dreary and sad. Isn't it funny how the sunshine makes us happy, even on a cold day? We often say, "It is cold out today, but the sun is out!" The sun has a way of warming us up, even when the temperature is cold.

Jesus will warm you up from the inside. When you ask Jesus to be your Savior, He comes into your life and warms you up, just like the sun warms the inside of a car, even on a cold day. He will brighten your outlook on life. He will bring joy and happiness into your life and the lives of those around you.

There is a gospel chorus I learned as a child and I remember my mother singing it often. *Heavenly sunshine, heavenly sunshine, flooding my soul with Glory divine. Heavenly sunshine, heavenly sunshine, Hallelujah, Jesus is mine.* When you belong to Jesus and Jesus belongs to you, you can have sunshine inside of you, no matter what the weather is like around you!

He shall be as the light of the morning; A cloudless sunrise. When the tender grass, springs forth upon the earth; As sunshine after rain.
2 Samuel 23:4 TLB

58

WHEN WE FACE A HOPELESS SITUATION WE PUT OUR HOPE IN GOD

Nehemiah is the Old Testament prophet who takes on the project of rebuilding the wall around Jerusalem. The situation looked hopeless. We sometimes find ourselves in situations where the wall of our defenses against the enemy has been knocked down, and we need a time of rebuilding or regrouping. We need to come back to our gracious Heavenly Father and spend more time with Him, leaning into His promises and recommitting our lives to His direction and care.

I have faced several hopeless situations in my life. When my husband and I owned our own business there were times when it looked like there was no way we would be able to recover financially from the situation we were in. At one point, our property was in foreclosure. But our God made a way for us to stay on our property, and eventually move from that area to another state. God helped us to *rebuild* in a new place.

If you find yourself in need of *rebuilding*, start by asking Jesus to be your Savior and give Him control of your life. Let Him do the heavy lifting of rebuilding. He wants to see you happy, healthy, and prosperous. When you commit your way to Jesus, He will guide you. Put your hope in God, the one who created you.

They said to me, "Things are not going well for those who returned to the province of Judah. They are in great trouble and disgrace. The wall of Jerusalem has been torn down, and the gates have been destroyed by fire." When I heard this, I sat down and wept. In fact, for days I mourned, fasted, and prayed to the God of heaven.
Nehemiah 1:3-4 NLT

59

JESUS LIVES, HE'S COMING BACK IF YOU WAIT, IT MAY BE TOO LATE

Our days on earth are limited. Some of us are given eighty or more years, others are not. My first experience with someone young dying, was when I was sixteen. My brother, who was thirty at the time, was killed in a motorcycle accident. I remember thinking young people were not supposed to die, only old people. But of course, it's not true. Young people die all the time. It may be by accident, illness, or unfortunately, when they take their own life. Jesus himself was only about thirty-three when he died for us on the cross.

Maybe you have a personal experience with someone young dying. Jesus comes for all of us. It may be when we are young or when we are old, but he will come and our life on earth will be over, the book closed. The only way we can be certain we will go to heaven is by asking Jesus to save us from our sin and from hell. He is the only way (John 14:6). Don't let the story of your life end in heartache for those you love. Ask Jesus to be your Savior so your eternal destination is heaven. In this way, your loved ones can know you will be united again.

Jesus has promised us He will take us to heaven to be with Him when we leave this earth if we have acknowledged Him as Lord of our life and Savior of our soul. We have only this brief moment in time, don't wait to ask Jesus into your life.

And all who trust him—God's Son—to save them have eternal life; those who don't believe and obey him shall never see heaven, but the wrath of God remains upon them.
John 3:36 TLB

60

HEAVEN, IT'S NOT WHAT YOU DO IT'S WHO YOU KNOW

If God had not concerned Himself with man, our world would be a different place. What if after Adam and Eve ate the fruit in the garden, God would have just thrown up His hands and said, "Well, that little experiment didn't work!", and turned His back on mankind. What a different world we would live in! Even though Adam and Eve made the wrong choice, God still loved them.

I am so glad God did not give up on mankind and does not give up on us today. When we mess up and make poor choices, all we need to do is come back to Him in repentance. He forgives, and forgets, and continues to love us. Adam and Eve knew God personally, they talked with him every day.

We can know God like that too. He wants to spend time with us each day. And one day, when we get to heaven, we will see Him face to face! Jesus tells us the only way to get to heaven is through Him. (John 14:6) Make sure you don't fall into the trap of trying to earn your way to heaven by what you do, and instead, spend time getting to know Jesus, your Savior. He is the Way, the Truth, and the Life. When you know Jesus, you know your final destination is heaven.

*—it is, remember, by grace and not by achievement
that you are saved—*
Ephesians 2:5 Phillips

THE CROSS

*Again he left them and prayed,
'My Father! If this cup cannot go away until I drink it all,
your will be done.'*

Matthew 26:42 TLB

61

LOVE AND FORGIVENESS CAME TOGETHER ON THE CROSS

Jesus died so our sins could be forgiven. God's love is so full of mercy and grace He does not want anyone to perish, but *all* to be saved. (2 Peter 3:9) The love of God and forgiveness Jesus offers came together in one moment on the cross when Jesus cried out, "It is finished!" (John 19:30). The work Jesus came to earth to do, was to show God to the people of Israel, and to all who would believe He was the son of God. He came so we could see God in action in our world. Jesus said He only did the work His Father told Him to do. (John 5:36) The culmination of that work was to die as the perfect sacrifice for our sins.

The human part of Jesus did not want to go through the pain and suffering of the crucifixion. But the God part of Him knew why He had come to earth and what was required of Him. He laid down His life for all of us. He forgave those who persecuted Him, and He loved them all. Sometimes I think it is harder to love than it is to forgive. To love people, we have to accept them as they are and forgive them when they need it.

Sometimes it takes an act of our will, and a lot of prayer to love those we feel have hurt us or those who appear to despise us. We must forgive when we have been offended or hurt. But we must go one step further and ask Jesus to put His love in our hearts for those who are difficult for us to love. What we are not able to do in our strength, we can do with the help of Jesus.

In him we have redemption through his blood, the forgiveness of sins, in accordance with the riches of God's grace.
Ephesians 1:7 NIV

62

THE POWER OF THE CROSS IS IN THE LOVE

Do you ever wear a cross necklace? Most ladies and some men who are Christians have a cross necklace. Some of us, like myself, have a good variety to choose from in different colors and styles! Some people I know wear a cross every day around their neck to remind them of what Jesus did for them on the cross.

Life is full of difficult seasons. Jesus says, *"Here on earth you will have many troubles and sorrows; but cheer up, for I have overcome the world."* John 16:33 TLB. What a blessing to share each day with the ONE who has overcome death, sickness, poverty, and lack and provides healing and wholeness in all areas of our lives. There is power in the blood Jesus shed for us on the cross. There is also extraordinary power in the love Jesus has for us. His love gave Him the ability to suffer and die for us. Cling to Jesus each day. Let the power of the cross and the power of His love overcome all of your trouble.

Next time you see a cross necklace, or you put one on yourself, think to yourself, *Jesus died for me because He loves ME!*

But God showed his great love for us by sending Christ to die for us while we were still sinners.
Romans 5:8 TLB

63

MERCY AND GRACE ARE FOUND AT THE CROSS

Mercy is when God does not give us what we deserve, for example, eternal death because of the sin in our lives. Grace is when God gives us what we don't deserve, for example, eternal life with Him in heaven. Without the work, Jesus did on the cross (and it WAS work, my friend), we would not have mercy and grace in our lives.

If Jesus had not died on the cross, if the enemy had convinced Him it was not worth the pain, and the agony, there would be no way for us to get to heaven without living a perfect life. But He was willing to die in our place and take OUR sin on Himself. When we trust in Him for our salvation, we can be certain, when we die, we will go to heaven to be with Him forever.

Mercy and grace are also active in our lives here on earth. Mercy is when you forget to put on your turn signal, or don't see the car in the lane beside you, and you DON'T have an accident! Yikes! Been there, done that! Grace is when you order the less expensive new carpet, but you get the better quality by mistake, and the salesman says, it's okay, you can just keep the better carpet! Bonus! Does God do things like that for His children? I like to think He does. He loves us, and He wants to bless us. Claim His wonderful mercy and grace today, if you have not already done so. Take a few minutes and remember some of the times when mercy and grace have shown up in your own life!

Let us then approach God's throne of grace with confidence, so that we may receive mercy and find grace to help us in our time of need.
Hebrews 4:16 NIV

64

FOR ALL YOU DO HIS BLOOD'S FOR YOU

You would not find this saying in an advertising campaign in our world! But maybe it would have appeared in Nazareth just after Jesus's resurrection! Do you think most of His followers understood the significance of His death and resurrection? Or do you think it took them years to put it all together? I wonder.

Jesus's blood, the blood He shed when He was wounded for our transgressions and died on the cross, is for you. It was shed to cover your sins, to take your punishment, the punishment you deserved, on himself, so you could live forever in heaven with all the saints and with God the father. Jesus knew, long before the time of His crucifixion, His blood was for you, to cover all your sins. He knew why He came and what His purpose was. He knew YOU, and He knew what you were capable of doing. Those nasty thoughts and actions, the things you wish had never happened, but somehow they did. He knew. He loves you so much He did not want you to die for your sin. Even today, He would do it again, for YOU!

Accept what He did for you, believe it was for YOU He died and for YOU he gave His life willingly. Give Him your life in return and see where He will lead you. You can have the assurance that one day you will be with Him in heaven.

But he was wounded and bruised for our sins. He was beaten that we might have peace; he was lashed—and we were healed!
Isaiah 53:5 TLB

65

IN A HURTING WORLD JESUS IS THE ULTIMATE HEALER

I do not know anyone who has not experienced hurt in some areas of life. There is physical, emotional, and spiritual hurt in our lives. Emotional pain can last much longer than physical pain. It can affect relationships and even a person's ability to work and function. Jesus knows how to heal all types of pain.

Do you know someone, or maybe you are someone, who has a deep hurt? Jesus wants to wipe away the pain. It is the enemy of our soul, Satan, who keeps reminding us of the bad things which happened in our lives. He reminds us of the times we failed or did not get it right. It is the enemy who wants us to be sick and in pain and sad and depressed. Jesus wants us healthy and happy. It's by his stripes we are healed. (Isaiah 53:5)

Jesus wants you well and whole in every area of your life. He wants you to have heart peace, and joy. He wants you to find contentment in your situation and to trust Him to be your provider and your healer. Spend some time today focusing on what Jesus has done for you on the cross, He did it all for you! Let His healing power be at work in your life.

Jesus turned and saw her. "Take heart, daughter," he said, "your faith has healed you." And the woman was healed at that moment.
Matthew 9:22 NIV

66

JESUS HUNG OUT WITH CRIMINALS

Jesus was not concerned at all about who His friends were. Not only did he die between two criminals, but he also spent a lot of time during his ministry with people who lived less than perfect lives. He associated with tax collectors and prostitutes. He associated with thieves and criminals of all types. He was more concerned about finding those who needed a Savior, than about those who were religious. He wants to see all men and women repent of their sins and give their lives to Him.

I find it interesting about the two thieves who were crucified with Jesus. One was willing to believe Jesus was the Messiah, the son of God. The other was not. Even though they were both sentenced to death for their actions, one went to heaven, the other to hell. Do you suppose the one who believed had been in the crowds listening to Jesus preach? Maybe some of his family were followers of Jesus. I would think this criminal knew something of who Jesus was before he ended up on a cross beside him on that Friday afternoon.

Jesus would have gladly accepted both of them in heaven, if the other thief would have been willing to acknowledge Jesus as the son of God. Don't miss your chance to ask Him to be your Savior, don't put off your decision, do it today!

Jesus answered him, 'Truly I tell you, today you will be with me in paradise.'
Luke 23:43 NIV

67

DON'T JUST SAY I LOVE YOU FIND A WAY TO SHOW IT, JESUS DID

How often do you say "I love you"? Do you tell your children? Your spouse? Your parents? Sometimes I tell my dog "I love you"! But how do I SHOW them I love them? The dog is probably the easiest! She knows I love her when I pet her or give her a special treat. She is a Golden Retriever, so she is by nature easy to please!

The people in my life are a little harder to convince by my actions. I can do nice things for them, or buy them gifts. I can go out of my way to put their needs ahead of mine. All of these things show my love for those people in my life who are dear to me. I know though, at times, my human nature and my desires to please myself overrule my desire to show my love. Those closest to us see the good and the bad in us. The important thing is for the loving actions to outweigh the times we are unloving or unkind. Those we are closest to will know if our words of love are true or false by our actions.

Jesus loved all of us so much He was willing to die the death of a criminal on the cross, even though he never committed a crime. He not only laid down His life for us, but He also did it in the most painful and humiliating way. He knows what it is to be wrongly accused. He knows the full range of emotions we experience as humans. Jesus showed us how to love. He KNOWS you. And He LOVES you! Keep trying to find ways to show your true love for others.

Don't just pretend to love others. Really love them. Hate what is wrong. Hold tightly to what is good.
Romans 12:9 NLT

68

TWO SIGNS OF A CHRISTIAN GIVING AND FORGIVING

If you are a Christian, you know the power of forgiveness. The forgiveness of God for our sin and the forgiveness we give others when they hurt us. It is not healthy to hold on to wrongs and hurts. Even something small can sometimes be difficult to forgive.

At one of my part-time jobs, one of the managers decided to give my locker to another employee. My locker number had not been written down when I was hired. I had some personal belongings in my locker. Rather than save them a few days to see if they belonged to someone, he just threw them away. Great! But it didn't feel so great. Imagine my surprise when I opened my locker and found someone else's purse and water bottle in my locker! Then to discover my belongings had just been thrown away. If it had been a plastic water bottle and a candy wrapper, no big deal. But it was a sweater, a coffee mug, and some additional items. I was hurt. I could have held on to anger over the situation, but I chose to forgive and let it go.

We live in a fallen world. It allows us to practice forgiveness. We can add to forgiveness by giving. When we not only forgive, but also give mercy, or something tangible, we spoil the plan of the enemy. There are times when we need to say *I forgive you*. Sometimes it is more important for the person doing the forgiving than for the person being forgiven. Take some time to practice the art of giving and forgiving.

O Lord, you are so good, so ready to forgive, so full of unfailing love for all who ask for your help.
Psalm 86:5 NLT

69

MY REDEEMER LIVES DO YOU KNOW HIM

Jesus is my redeemer. Do you know Him as your redeemer too? There is a song titled *There is a Redeemer,* written by Keith and Melody Green. Some of you reading this may be old enough to remember some of their songs. This song talks about Jesus our Redeemer, the one who saved us from having to die for our sins. Jesus took our place when He died on the cross all those years ago. He not only died for those living in his day but for everyone who would ask Him to be their personal redeemer.

To be redeemed means we don't have to suffer for our sins. We don't have to go to hell, even though we deserve the punishment. We are all sinners. None of us lives a perfect life. We all mess up at times and do things, or say things, we should not do or say. It is the sinful nature in all of us. Jesus died to redeem us from the punishment for our sin. If you know Jesus as your Lord and your Savior, you know you have a friend and a redeemer who will always be there for you.

Take some time today to think about the areas in your life that are not perfect. Ask Jesus to forgive you, then thank Him for being your redeemer, taking your place on the cross and dying for your sins.

Our Redeemer, whose name is the Lord of Heaven's Armies, is the Holy One of Israel.
Isaiah 47:4 NLT

70

THE CROSS OF CHRIST CHANGED THE WORLD LET IT CHANGE YOU

When you prepare for Easter, are you more like Mary who was MOST interested in what Jesus had to say? Or more like Martha who was MOST interested in having a wonderful meal for her friends? Often as women, we tend to think about the Easter dinner, or the kids' Easter baskets, or maybe the new Easter clothes. Those things are most like Martha, of course. The Mary part of us would answer, "Yes, my heart is ready to celebrate Jesus, my risen Lord, and Savior!"

When you prepare for Easter Sunday this year I would challenge you to spend as much time reading the Easter story in the Gospels, and asking God to do a work in your heart, as you spend planning and preparing for the rest of the holiday. The book of John is a great place to read about the week before the crucifixion and resurrection. All four gospels have the Easter story recorded. Make sure you read all of it, not just a part of the story.

When you really think about it, the short period in time from the Passover supper to the discovery of the empty tomb did indeed change the world. It opened up the way for us to *come boldly to the throne of Grace* (Hebrews 4). As you open your heart to receive all Christ has done for you, let the miracle of Jesus resurrection change your life as well.

But the Lord answered her, "Martha, my dear, you are worried and bothered about providing so many things. Only a few things are really needed, perhaps only one. Mary has chosen the best part and you must not tear it away from her!"
Luke 10:41-42 Phillips

THANKSGIVING

Bless the Lord, O my soul, And forget not all His benefits.

Psalm 103:2 NKJV

71

GIVE THANKS TO GOD WITHOUT HIM WE CAN'T BREATHE

Each person at rest, breathes about 23,000 breaths a day. And we take all those breaths without thinking about it. God is the one who *breathed* life into each of us. (Genesis 2:7) When we stop breathing, we die. There are SO many things in this life to be thankful for. But without breathing, we are not able to enjoy any of them.

Recently, one of my friends who has COPD was in the hospital again. He was not able to breathe on his own, so he had a tube inserted to allow a machine to breathe for him. Praise God he recovered and is growing stronger each day. But he would be the first to agree we should thank God for the ability to breathe on our own.

What are some things you are thankful for today? You can make a list. On the days when you are not feeling very thankful, you can take out your list and remind yourself. If you have trouble keeping track of your list, try taping it inside one of your kitchen cabinet doors. Maybe you want to put it on your refrigerator as a reminder to everyone in your family to be thankful. Keep breathing!

The Spirit of God has made me;
the breath of the Almighty gives me life.
Job 33:4 NIV

72

COUNT YOUR BLESSINGS
IT WILL MAKE YOU SMILE

Have you had any good news lately? Sometimes it is easy to focus on the bad news of life, rather than the good news. I think our world (with the news media and internet) tends to keep us focused on what is *wrong* rather than on what is *right*. It takes effort at times to count our blessings and look for the good things each day.

You can try this little exercise; at the end of each day, ask your spouse, or a friend, "What is the worst thing that happened to you today?" Then ask, "What is the best thing that happened to you today?" The questions should be answered for today only. When we end with the best thing, it makes us realize every day has some good things in it. The more we focus on what is good and positive the happier we will be. Counting your blessings is sure to make you thankful, and thankfulness will make you smile!

And now, dear brothers and sisters, one final thing. Fix your thoughts on what is true, and honorable, and right, and pure, and lovely, and admirable. Think about things that are excellent and worthy of praise.
Philippians 4:8 NLT

73

GOD HAS TWO DWELLINGS ONE IN HEAVEN AND ONE IN A THANKFUL HEART

Do you have a thankful heart? What exactly does it mean to have a thankful heart? I think it means to be looking for the things we can be thankful for each day. God does dwell in a thankful heart. It says in the Bible God inhabits our praises. (Psalm 22:3) Isn't it wonderful to know! When you want God to come closer to you, praise, and thank Him!

If you are feeling down, and kind of grumpy, try to think of something to be thankful for. Each morning I am thankful I can get out of bed and go to work. Sometimes I am not thrilled that I have to work Monday through Friday. I think I could sure use more vacation! But then I remember those who are not able to work, or can't find suitable work. It is a hard life if you are not able to work each day. God created us to have a purpose, and most of us find it in our work. If you are a Mom at home, each day brings a new opportunity to thank God for your children. If they are healthy, well-fed, and clothed, it is something to be thankful for.

But most of all, I am thankful Jesus is the Lord of my life and I can trust Him to lead and guide me each day. Let Jesus dwell in your heart and be thankful!

Devote yourselves to prayer with an alert mind and a thankful heart.
Colossians 4:2 NLT

74

THANK GOD EVERY DAY IS A NEW BEGINNING

When you woke up this morning, were you thinking about the past, the future, or today? I generally start thinking about what is ahead of me today. There are times though when I get stuck thinking about the past, but the past can't be changed. And there are times I spend too much time thinking about the future, since I truly do not know what will happen even in the next hour.

Every day starts as a fresh beginning. God is able to work mighty miracles in your life and turn your life around if necessary. I believe He is the God of the turn-around. I see it many places in the Bible, Joseph in prison (Genesis chapter 39). Job from everything, to nothing, to twice as much as before (Job chapters 1, 2, and 43). The three Hebrews in the fiery furnace (Daniel chapter 3). Paul and Silas in stocks in prison (Acts chapter 16). So many times God takes what looks like a very bad situation and turns it into something good.

If, as you look forward, you cannot see anything good on the horizon, remember, each day is a new day and God can change your situation today! Nothing is impossible with Him. Thank Him for the good things in your life today, and trust Him for your tomorrow.

"Well, look!" Nebuchadnezzar shouted. "I see four men, unbound, walking around in the fire, and they aren't even hurt by the flames! And the fourth looks like a god!"
Daniel 3:25 TLB

75

DON'T FORGET TO THANK GOD FOR WHAT HE HAS DONE FOR YOU

I try to start my day by thanking God for another day to do the things He has called me to do. No matter what you are doing, you should consider it your calling. Are you working on an assembly line? In a retail store? As a delivery person? Whatever you are doing most likely you will come in contact with others during your day. God has something for you to do every day. Thank Him for the way He is at work in your life and look for the things He wants you to do.

There are times in life when it is easy to be thankful for all our blessings, and there are times when it is much more difficult. The Bible encourages us to give the *sacrifice* of praise, our lips giving thanks (Hebrews 13:15). There are times when life is hard and it is more challenging to be thankful. Sometimes it seems like a sacrifice to us to give up our negative attitude and change our thinking to be thankful instead.

When we think about all the things God has done for us, just by his willingness to come to earth and die for us, we should experience a sense of thanksgiving in our hearts. If Jesus had not willingly laid down His life for us, none of us would be going to heaven. It was His love for us that made the difference. So be thankful this week as you do your daily tasks. Be thankful for having something to do, and someone (Jesus) who loves you more than you can ever understand. Be thankful.

And whatever you do, do it heartily, as to the Lord and not to men.
Colossians 3:23 NKJV

76

GIVE THANKS TO GOD FOR SOMETHING TODAY

Each day is a new day to thank God for all of the blessings in your life. Even when we are going through difficult times, there is ALWAYS something to be thankful for. If we have food to eat and clothes to wear, we are blessed. You may also be thankful for the relationships in your life. Your spouse, your children, your parents, brothers and sisters, and extended family. You can always be thankful for your relationship with Jesus.

Often our days can blend together, one day being very much the same as the next. We should not always look for spectacular moments. Rather pay attention to the simple moments where God shows up and is with you, helping you to reach others, one at a time. God sometimes uses the smallest things in our lives to bring Him glory. Not long ago, I had extra tickets for a concert at our church. I had purchased them for friends who were not able to come. I was able to pass them on to one of my co-workers and his Mom at a deep discount. Not a big thing, but a blessing to them. We can be thankful for each *God moment* we encounter.

Find something to be thankful for each day. It will lighten your mood and lift your spirits. God is so good, all of the time!

How great is the goodness you have stored up for those who fear you.
You lavish it on those who come to you for protection,
blessing them before the watching world.
Psalm 31:19 NLT

77

TRUE THANKS IS FROM THE HEART NOT JUST THE MOUTH

Have you ever said "Thank you", and not meant it? I'm thinking of the gift you received, the one you really didn't like much, but you said "Thank you", because you knew it was the right thing to say. How often do we thank God for our daily bread by saying a table prayer we have memorized? Do we engage our minds when we pray, or is it just words?

If you really want to express your thanks, it has to come from your heart. Heart *thanks* is different than *mouth thanks*. When you say "thank you" from the heart it is because you are truly grateful. Sometimes deep thankfulness comes with tears. Our emotions get involved as well as our minds. It is good to experience this type of thankfulness from time to time.

You can practice being thankful from your heart by looking around at what you already have. We are rich people in so many ways. You may not consider yourself rich compared to others you know, but there are many in the world with far less than we have. Thank God from your heart for your many blessings today. He is the giver of every good and perfect gift.

Whatever is good and perfect is a gift coming down to us from God our Father, who created all the lights in the heavens.
He never changes or casts a shifting shadow.
James 1:17 NLT

78

THANKSGIVING BELONGS TO GOD HE IS OUR ULTIMATE PROVIDER

We are all so blessed to know the real source of all the good things in our lives. Thanksgiving for me is more than just a few days off from work in November. It is a time to reflect on the blessings God has provided for me and my family during the year. Knowing God is my source in every situation helps so much to take away some of the stress of life. I know I can always trust Him to lead and guide me through whatever challenges I may face.

God is such a good provider. There is a Writer's Conference I like to attend not far from my home. It was held for the first time in the summer of 2017. In the fall, the early registration came out with a discounted price for the following summer. The day registration began, I had received some extra money for extra work. I was able to use it to register for the conference. God's timing was again perfect and He showed Himself as my provider that day. I was so thankful!

I know God knows my needs before I even ask (Matthew 6:8). I know nothing that happens in my life is a surprise to Him. He is always with me. The angels are watching over me every moment. God is with you too and watches over you. Why do we ever wonder about how things will turn out? Trust God for your every need. He is our ultimate provider.

For God is the one who provides seed for the farmer and then bread to eat. In the same way, he will provide and increase your resources and then produce a great harvest of generosity in you.
2 Corinthians 9:10 NLT

79

MAKE THANKS-LIVING A WAY OF LIFE

It seems to me Thanksgiving is a forgotten holiday. Christmas seems to have overtaken it, due to the push of retailers to sell more. After all, there is not much money to be made off of Thanksgiving, except at grocery stores! Thanksgiving should be a time of remembering all of the things we are thankful for in our lives.

For me, Thanksgiving is just as important as Christmas. In fact, Christmas is a type of Thanksgiving for me. I am always so THANKFUL for what God has done in my life and the things He continues to do each day. I am so thankful Jesus left His place in heaven and came to earth to live as one of us, to take our sin on Himself and pay the price that had to be paid. I always want to nurture a thankful heart toward God and others around me.

Instead of celebrating Thanksgiving for a few days at the end of November, make Thanksgiving a way of life. I like to call it, Thanks-Living!

And let the peace that comes from Christ rule in your hearts. For as members of one body you are called to live in peace.
And always be thankful.
Colossians 3:15 NLT

80

A THANKFUL HEART LEADS TO A CONTENTED LIFE

Have you ever written out your prayers for your family? Or maybe just a prayer of thankfulness to our wonderful Savior, Jesus. If not, I would encourage you to try it. It is great to be able to go back and read those prayers from time to time. I have found the more thankful I am, the more content I am. Here is my prayer for you at Thanksgiving:

Lord Jesus, first of all, thank you for saving us while we were yet sinners. Thank you for redeeming us and cleansing us from ALL our sins. Thank you, you see us for who we really are, and still love us.

Let the time each of us spends with family be peaceful and filled with your love. If there are those in our family circle who don't know you, may there be opportunities to talk about your love and your saving grace. For those who are traveling, protect them, and bring them back safely. For those who are hosting a gathering, help them with every detail, and help them to have a wonderful time with those gathered around their table. Most of all Jesus, we lift up our thanks and praise to you for all you have done for us, our Savior, and our Helper. Amen.

Give thanks to the Lord for He is good, His faithful love endures forever.
Psalm 106:1 NLT

CHRISTMAS

For there is born to you this day in the city of David a Savior, who is Christ the Lord.

Luke 2:11 NKJV

81

JESUS IS THE REASON FOR THE SEASON

We started the sign ministry beside the highway just before Christmas in 1997. This familiar Christmas message was the first message we put out. A few years earlier we had started a home-based business. We knew when we put up the big black road signs with the pink letters and the faith message on them, we would lose some business because of them. We also knew God was in control, of our business, and our lives as well. We continued to put a message of hope and encouragement on the road signs until we moved in the fall of 2014. Many of the short sayings in this book are the sayings that appeared on the signs.

I heard a great Christmas message about the shepherds who were out in the field the first Christmas night. Some of them were probably tired of their job and did not want to be there, but what a blessing to see the Heavenly Host and hear the birth announcement for Jesus our Savior. What if one of them had stayed home that night, or quit the day before? They would have missed out on one of history's greatest events. Sometimes when we are not where we want to be, God has a blessing in it for us. If you are doing what God has called you to do, don't quit.

I hope this Christmas season will include some great events where Jesus is the central focus. Keep Jesus in the center of your celebration, remember He is the reason we HAVE the season!

That night there were shepherds staying in the fields nearby, guarding their flocks of sheep.... Suddenly, the angel was joined by a vast host of others—the armies of heaven—praising God...
Luke 2: 8 and 13 NLT

82

IS JESUS ON YOUR CHRISTMAS LIST GIVE HIM YOUR HEART

Do you make a Christmas list each year as I do? Listing the names of each of those you want to give a gift to? Jesus should be on your list if He is not.

December is one of our cold months in the north. But we can also have sunny mild weather at times in the winter. If you live in a northern climate, then Christmas comes in the winter. As we approach the Christmas season, what is the condition of your heart? Is it warming up? Or is your heart cold toward Jesus? I know in our culture, it is sometimes difficult to stay focused on the WHY of Christmas. We all know the sayings *Jesus is the Reason for the Season*, and *Without Christ, there would be no Christmas*, but today I would like you to examine the condition of your heart.

Is your heart full of love for Jesus, your family, and those around you? Is it the love of Jesus that motivates you to give at Christmas, or is it something else? Take a few minutes right now to search your heart and ask God to show you anything that may need changing. This Christmas make sure your heart belongs to Jesus.

Wherever your treasure is, there the desires of your heart will also be.
Matthew 6:21 NLT

83

JESUS GAVE THE GREATEST GIFT HE GAVE HIS LIFE TO SET US FREE

As the season of Christmas comes closer, many of us begin to think about purchasing Christmas gifts for family and friends. Have you started your shopping yet? I am generally a *little by little* Christmas shopper. Some people are all about the thrill of the last minute or the big sale. Some like to find just the right gift for everyone on their list. No matter what type you are, giving gifts at Christmas should be a blessing to both the giver and the receiver. Isn't it great to know we serve a God who always cares about the small things in our lives, like finding just the right gift for someone we care about! You can pray and ask God what gift you should give the people on your list.

God gave us the perfect gift when He gave His son. Jesus gave us the ultimate gift by giving His life so we could go to heaven. God has given each of us gifts as well. Some of us are preachers or evangelists, others are group leaders or have a gift of serving, or making beautiful music. See Romans chapter 12 for a list of gifts given to each of us. Whatever gifts God has given you, use them to bring Glory to Him all year long. It is the best way we can honor Him for the gift He gave us.

God has given each of you a gift from his great variety of spiritual gifts. Use them well to serve one another.
I Peter 4:10 NLT

84
SEEK HIS PRESENCE NOT HIS PRESENTS

When I am out and about in the stores and shops during the Christmas season, I make a point of saying "Merry Christmas!" I know there are other holidays celebrated by other cultures at the same time. It does not offend me if someone says "Happy Hanukkah!" in return. I understand they are Jewish and it is what they are celebrating. I am a Christian, and I am celebrating Christmas, so rather than Happy Holiday's, I prefer wishing others a Merry Christmas!

Speaking of Christmas, it is time to draft my annual Christmas letter to my family and friends, which will, as always, include our testimony of how good God has been to us over the year, and a wish for them to know Jesus personally. I know many of my Christian friends include something about Jesus in their Christmas letters as a witness to their family and friends. If it is your habit also, then, good for you! We should be careful at Christmas time to keep Jesus at the center of our lives and our homes. It is good to seek His presence at this time of year, and all through the year, rather than His presents!

They (the wise men) entered the house and saw the child with his mother, Mary, and they bowed down and worshiped him. Then they opened their treasure chests and gave him gifts of gold, frankincense, and myrrh.
Matthew 2:11 NLT

85

TAKE TIME TO WORSHIP THE KING OF KINGS

As I began to write my Christmas letter one year, I was not sure what to write. *I got a new job and my husband and I are separated.* That would leave the wrong impression! During the year I had taken a new job 200 miles from the town we lived in, and my husband had not been able to join me yet. So, I was struggling a bit with our Christmas letter. How can I be positive and truthful, and deliver God's message of hope and comfort to my friends and relatives? But I persisted, and got the letter written. I chose to focus on the positive, rather than the negative.

Recently I have been thinking about all of the hurting people at Christmas. The season seems to have a way of magnifying the hurts, losses, and struggles of life. In one family, someone may be near death, in another, there may be not enough money for a Christmas dinner, much less gifts. In yet another family there may be strife and hurt between family members. I think it is because our society expects us to put on a *happy* face for the holiday. It makes our hurts seem bigger at this time of year.

We need to turn our focus off of ourselves and put it on Jesus, the King of Kings. When we take time to worship Him, then we understand our problems are small in the grand history of the world. I pray your Christmas family traditions will help you to focus on Jesus, the King of Kings and Lord of Lords who reigns forever and ever.

On his robe and thigh was written this title:
"King of Kings and Lord of Lords."
Revelation 19:16 TLB

86

WITHOUT JESUS THERE WOULD BE NO CHRISTMAS

Christmas is less than two weeks away. I wonder where Mary was two weeks before the birth of Jesus. On the road to Bethlehem? I'm sure she was not very excited about that trip! Such a long way, and very pregnant, and young, with a man she probably did not know very well, and a smelly donkey. Although she was probably thankful for the donkey, even if he did smell! But they had to go to Bethlehem to fulfill the prophecy (Micah 5:2). If Jesus had never been born, we would not have Christmas.

Where are you today on the road of your life? Closer to Jesus than you were at this time last year? Or are you farther away? What course corrections do you need to make in the year ahead to keep your life on the right path?

Spend some time asking Jesus what He wants for you in the year ahead. Then, when He tells you something, write it down on a little sticky note or something similar and put it in your Bible. Let it be your map for the coming year.

Joseph went up from the town of Nazareth in Galilee to David's town, Bethlehem, in Judea, because he was a direct descendant of David, to be registered with his future wife, Mary, now in the later stages of her pregnancy.
Luke 2: 4-5 Phillips

87

THIS CHRISTMAS PAY MORE ATTENTION TO PEOPLE THAN THINGS

Are you ready for Christmas? We hear this question often in December. But we usually answer based on whether or not we have the cards and letters sent, the gifts bought and wrapped and the menu for Christmas dinner prepared. We don't often answer based on the condition of our hearts. Is your heart ready to receive Jesus?

What if Jesus would come FOR YOU today? What if we KNEW Jesus was coming to our house this Christmas? My Dad had a little business size card he kept by his bedside, it simply said, *Perhaps Today, Jesus will come*. It was a daily reminder for him to live his life like it may be his last day. It is indeed the "Blessed Hope" we all look for (Titus 2:13), the day when Jesus will return for His church and we will be caught up in the air to be with him (1 Thessalonians 4:17).

When you think about it, does it matter if the house is decorated just right, or the cookies baked or the presents bought and wrapped? Well, yes, it matters, but we need to make sure we keep things in the right order. Nothing matters MORE than our relationship with Jesus and with our families. I like to say, "Anything can happen any time, better be ready to meet Jesus". So this Christmas, be ready. Be ready to meet Jesus, be ready to invite him into your home and heart, and be ready to tell others about how special He is to you!

Then, together with them, we who are still alive and remain on the earth will be caught up in the clouds to meet the Lord in the air. Then we will be with the Lord forever.
I Thessalonians 4:17 NLT

88

GOD GAVE US HIS ONLY SON WILL YOU GIVE HIM YOUR LIFE

Christmas is a time for giving and receiving. There is a saying, not in the Bible I might add, it is more blessed to give than to receive. I disagree with that idea. I believe they are equally blessed. Both giving and receiving bless the giver and the receiver. Unexpected gifts are usually a real blessing!

My husband and I were not blessed with children. So for many years now, at Christmas time I have adopted a family in need and provided Christmas gifts for them. I know they are blessed to receive Christmas gifts when their resources were lacking. I know I am equally blessed to be able to give with a joyful heart at this time of year.

God is the one who has taught us to be givers by giving the ultimate gift of His son Jesus. When you receive Jesus into your heart, you are completing the transaction. You see, it is not possible to give if there is no one to receive. So if you have not taken a step of faith yet, to give your life to Jesus, then prayerfully consider it today. When you give your life to Jesus, He will receive you as His own dear child and watch over and protect you all of your days.

This is how much God loved the world: He gave his Son, his one and only Son. And this is why: so that no one need be destroyed; by believing in him, anyone can have a whole and lasting life.
John 3:16 MSG

89

DON'T CROSS CHRIST OUT OF CHRISTMAS

Have you ever seen the greeting Merry X-Mas? When I was growing up, we did not use that form of the word Christmas in our household. We believed it was equivalent to crossing Christ out of Christmas. I searched the internet and found out the letter X can stand for the word Christ in Greek. But personally, I have not seen it used in any other combination except with Christmas.

Whether you use the abbreviated form of the word Christmas or not, please make sure to keep Christ in your Christmas celebration. Our commercialized celebration of the holiday may make it a challenge to remember why we celebrate the season. If you take a little time though and consider how you celebrate, you will see it is not hard to include Christ at your Christmas table, with a prayer of thanksgiving before the meal. To include Him around your Christmas tree by reading the Christmas story from the Bible, and to include Him by spending time going to church with your family.

Most of all I want to encourage you to keep Christ at the center of your life all year long. Not just at Christmas.

The angel replied, "The Holy Spirit will come upon you, and the power of the Most High will overshadow you. So the baby to be born will be holy, and he will be called the Son of God."
Luke 1:35 NLT

90

JESUS WAS BORN TO DIE
HE CAME BECAUSE OF YOU

YOU are SO special! Yes, YOU my friend! Christmas and Easter are not far apart on the calendar, but we don't often think of them at the same time. We really should. Jesus was born into our world so he could take our punishment for our sins on the cross. He was born to die.

I always find it amazing Jesus came to earth as an infant in his mother's womb, so he would have the entire human experience. God could have dropped him on earth as a twelve-year-old, but He did not. He was born into a family and raised by his mother and father. He had brothers and sisters and learned a trade. He wanted to identify with you and me. He wanted to know what it was like to live as we live here on earth.

My wish for you this Christmas is for you to have the peace and joy in your heart only Jesus can give. I want you to understand fully, His coming to earth was for YOU! I hope you can find a few quiet moments to sit in the presence of your Savior and thank Him for coming to earth.

Merry Christmas!

But when the set time had fully come, God sent his Son, born of a woman, born under the law, to redeem those under the law, that we might receive adoption to sonship.
Galatians 4:4-5 NIV

NEW YEAR / NEW BEGINNING

*And the one sitting on the throne said,
'See, I am making all things new!*

Revelation 21:5 TLB

91

START THE NEW YEAR RIGHT
PUT JESUS FIRST IN YOUR LIFE

Don't you just love a new year?! Jesus is all about new beginnings. When we accept Him as our Savior, He wipes away our past and gives us a fresh start. All of the old mess is forgotten. No matter what kind of year you had last year, you have a new beginning this year! Each day is a new beginning.

If your past has been filled with difficulties, then you may think your future has to be the same. Sometimes our past experiences color our expectations for the future. The Bible tells us a different story. Our God is the God of the turn-around. Consider Paul and Silas in jail (Acts chapter 16). They had been beaten and put in stocks, they were certainly uncomfortable, in pain, and likely hungry. Rather than moan and groan about the situation they were in, they started praising God. They were singing so loud the other prisoners could hear them. Suddenly there was an earthquake! Well, where do you think that came from? I'm sure the angels were having a great time shaking the place! It says the earthquake was so strong not only Paul and Silas were freed, but all of the other prisoners too! Did you know you can impact those around you by praising God every day?

As this New Year begins, don't neglect your time with God every day. Read the word, and sing songs of praise to Him, every day of the year!

Suddenly, there was a massive earthquake, and the prison was shaken to its foundations. All the doors immediately flew open, and the chains of every prisoner fell off!
Acts 16:26 NLT

92

NEW DAY PLANNER
PUT TIME WITH JESUS ON EVERY PAGE

Time moves on at a steady pace. Days turn into months and months turn into years. I was talking with a friend recently who had a particularly rough year. She said she would be really glad to see this year end. She was looking forward to a better year next year.

Sometimes life is difficult. But, while listening to a recent sermon, the pastor said "Expect only the BEST." Sometimes I think my expectations need an adjustment. The old saying, 'Blessed is he who expects nothing, for he shall not be disappointed', is just not true when we walk the life of faith in Jesus. When we are walking hand in hand with Jesus, we should instead expect ONLY the BEST!

Jesus delights to give us good things. It is good to pray daily for the favor of God in our lives and to expect good things from our loving Heavenly Father. Spend time each day this year with Jesus. Make it your priority. And whatever situation you find yourself in today, start expecting only God's best for you!

He fills my life with good things.
My youth is renewed like the eagles!
Psalm 103:5 NLT

93

DON'T DELAY
ASK JESUS TO CHANGE YOUR LIFE TODAY

Jesus is always ready to hear our confession. Why do we hold back when we have messed up? Sometimes I think it is because we have often been put down or criticized by others for the things we have done wrong. Jesus will not treat us that way. He wants us to come to him and confess the things we have done wrong so we can receive forgiveness and let go of the past. He is closer to us than any human being and will be more gentle and kind to us than anyone we know.

Jesus wants to change your life in the most wonderful way! He wants to give you good things. He wants to give you a new beginning. He wants to clean up the messes we all make. He wants to see us successful and healed and whole. Did you know the word Shalom means *nothing missing, nothing broken*? It is the word not only for peace, but for wholeness. Jesus wants us to have wholeness in our lives.

You do not need to be afraid to come to Him. The changes He has in mind for you will be for your good. He wants to give you a *hope and a future* full of blessings! So what are you waiting for?

For I know the plans I have for you," says the Lord. "They are plans for good and not for disaster, to give you a future and a hope. In those days when you pray, I will listen. If you look for me wholeheartedly, you will find me".
Jeremiah 29:11-13 NLT

94

OTHERS SEE WHAT YOU WANT THEM TO GOD SEES YOUR HEART

Is this message a comfort to you? Or a little bit scary? For some of us, it is easy to fool others into believing everything is *fine* with us. We smile, we talk about the weather, we say everything is going well. It's possible, everything is falling apart and you just don't want to admit it to those who are only occasional friends.

There are some people in our lives we really don't want to share all the deep issues with. They just want to fix us or tell us their best way of handling the situation. We have been down that road before and we know where it ends up.

God sees your heart, your innermost feelings, joys, fears, worries, and successes. God weeps with you when you are sad and rejoices with you when you are celebrating! He knows when you are fine and when you are NOT *fine*. He wants to be your source for ALL things, emotional, spiritual, physical, and financial. And most of all, He wants you to finish your life well and come home to be with Him, when the time is right.

As this new season begins, spend some time being honest with yourself and with God, let Him see ALL of you!

Mark well that God doesn't miss a move you make;
he's aware of every step you take.
Proverbs 5:21 MSG

95

IF GOD HAD A WALLET YOUR PICTURE WOULD BE IN IT

It's probably good God doesn't have a wallet, I can't even imagine how big it would have to be to hold all of those pictures! But just think, you are a child of God! Doesn't every parent carry pictures of their children? We are more likely today to have those pictures on our phones than in our wallets. Most likely God has a system something like that, where He can just call up any picture He is interested in at any time. Pictures of you when you were born, and when you made your parents proud. A picture of you on the wonderful day when you asked Him to be your Lord and Savior. Maybe a picture of you and your spouse on your wedding day when you joined your lives together so two could become one and create a new family.

He loves you more than you can ever know. He loves you on your good days, and on your bad days too. He knows you, better than you know yourself at times. If you ask Him, He is always willing to show you new things about yourself.

If your earthly parents were not very good examples of loving parents, then it may be hard to understand how much God loves you. Spend some time seeking out the verses in the Bible that talk about the love of God. It says in the Bible God IS love (I John 4:8). He personifies love. When you begin to understand God from reading His word, you will begin to understand what real love is like.

The Lord passed in front of Moses, calling out, "Yahweh! The Lord! The God of compassion and mercy! I am slow to anger and filled with unfailing love and faithfulness".
Exodus 34:6 NLT

96

SAY YES TO JESUS
MAKE IT YOUR FINAL ANSWER

There used to be a TV show on during prime time called *Who wants to be a Millionaire* The contestants had to answer a series of questions to win money. They were asked, "Is that your final answer?" At the judgment seat of Christ, you will no longer have an option to change your answer. You have your lifetime here on earth to make your final decision about eternity. When you say *yes* to the question 'Is Jesus your Lord and Savior?' you put Him in control of your life. Then Jesus IS your final answer!

It says in the Bible there will come a day when all of us stand before God and must answer for the life we lived here on earth. To some He will say, *Enter into my kingdom* and to others, *Depart from me, I never knew you.* (Matthew 25:31-46) Don't leave this earth before deciding to make Jesus your Lord and Savior. He wants everyone to choose Him. You may think you can put off making a choice. However NOT choosing Jesus is still choosing, it is choosing not to spend eternity with Him. Anything can happen to you at any time, there is no time like the present to make your decision. Let today be a new beginning for you. Make today the day you say YES to Jesus.

Then the King will say to those on his right, 'Come, you who are blessed by my Father; take your inheritance, the kingdom prepared for you since the creation of the world.'
Matthew 25:34 NIV

97

ONLY JESUS CAN SUPER GLUE BROKEN LIVES TOGETHER

Have you ever broken something very special to you? I have a set of salt and pepper shakers from my great-grandmother. They are birds with bonnets on, a male and a female. They have rhinestone eyes and are very colorful. They are special to me because they belonged to my great-grandmother, who I never met. One of them broke one day. When something is special, you don't throw it away because it breaks in a few places. No, you get out the super glue and put it back together to the best of your ability. It will not be perfect, but it will be whole.

Broken lives leave scars. Jesus told us *in this world you will have trouble.* (John 16:33 NIV) I don't know anyone who has not had trouble in their life. Some trouble is more difficult to overcome than others, but we all experience it in one form or another. There is a BUT in the words of Jesus though, he adds on, *But be of good cheer, for I have overcome the world!* Jesus is able to take our broken lives and put them back together. When we give control of our life to Him, He sets our feet on the right path and gives us a new start. He super glues us back together so we can continue on and help others along the way.

Do you know someone today, maybe someone close to you, who needs Jesus to put their broken life back together? My prayer is they will find healing for their hurts and a new beginning as they put their trust in Jesus.

He heals the brokenhearted and bandages their wounds.
Psalm 147:3 NLT

98

IF YOU DON'T LOVE PEOPLE YOU CAN'T LOVE JESUS

How are you doing with loving others? It may be difficult to love some of your family. Or maybe you are one of the fortunate ones who have fantastic relatives! The more you are around someone, the more you see their good side and their bad side. We live in a sin-filled world and ALL of us have times when we are not very loveable.

Think for a while about what it must have been like to be one of the disciples, called by Jesus to follow him. They saw him every day. They saw him hungry and thirsty, tired and worn out, frustrated, and even angry at times, but they never saw him sin. I'm sure they saw him laugh a lot, and teach at every opportunity. They saw him heal diseases like leprosy and blindness and raise people from the dead! Jesus was God with skin on. And God IS love, so Jesus loved the people he met. Even Peter after he denied him, Jesus still loved him, so very much. (John chapter 21)

Each day is a new opportunity to show the love of Jesus to those around us. They might be our family, our co-workers, or the people we meet during the day. If you find yourself rather tired and short-tempered some days, ask Jesus to let His love flow through you. When we walk with Jesus, we don't have to do it all on our own. He wants to help us love others the way He loves them. The more time you spend with Jesus, the easier it becomes to love others.

After breakfast, Jesus said to Simon Peter, "Simon, son of John, do you love me more than these?" "Yes, Master, you know I love you." Jesus said, "Feed my lambs."
John 21:15 MSG

99

JESUS HAS THE KEYS
WHAT DOOR DO YOU NEED HIM TO OPEN

One of my favorite verses is from Isaiah 46:11. In The Message paraphrase it says, *I'm in this for the long haul, I'll do exactly what I set out to do,' .... I've said it, and I'll most certainly do it. I've planned it, so it's as good as done.'* What can you apply this promise to in your life? God has planned it, so it's as good as done. What God has planned, no man can change.

Jesus holds the keys to your hopes and dreams. He will help you to accomplish all He has planned for your life when you let him. When you belong to Him, He is the author of your life story. He has things He wants you to accomplish. If you are not sure what those things are, ask Him.

Sometimes it may look like the things we are hoping for won't happen. In fact, sometimes they don't, at least not the way we thought they would, but when we commit our way to the Lord, we can trust Him. No matter how things work out, they are a part of His big and perfect plan for us. And we know He loves us SO much, He will always do the right thing for us. Whatever door you need opened today, ask Jesus to unlock it for you!

But the Lord's plans stand firm forever;
his intentions can never be shaken.
Psalm 33:11 NLT

100

P U S H
PRAY UNTIL SOMETHING HAPPENS

When you struggle with a decision or you need a miracle, apply the **PUSH** principle. Pray Until Something Happens. Don't pray until you feel like giving up. And don't pray until you are tired of praying. Keep on praying until you see the answer come.

Elijah had to keep praying. It had not rained for a very long time. (I Kings 18: 42-46) Elijah determined to pray. His servant was with him. Elijah would pray, and then ask his servant to go and look. Elijah did not quit praying when the report was no clouds, he just kept on praying, and every so often told his servant to go and look. Finally there was a small cloud. At the smallest encouragement, Elijah knew a big rainstorm was coming. God gave Elijah supernatural power to outrun the storm!

As the New Year begins, if you find yourself feeling a bit let down after the holidays, consider having a personal Praise-A-Thon! You can Praise Until Something Happens! Praise and prayer go together. Some mornings on my way to work, I just sing praises.

As we reflect on the past year it is important to thank God for all He has done. For the times He has carried us through, the times He has prompted us to act, and the times He has been patient with us. What a wonderful and merciful God He is! Whatever the year ahead holds, stay close to Jesus by reading His word and spending time with Him in prayer.

The seventh time the servant reported,
'A cloud as small as a man's hand is rising from the sea.'
I Kings 18:44a NIV

ABOUT THE AUTHOR

Lisa Donelson and her husband Tom owned and operated Trinity Trailers Sales in Floodwood, MN, the location of the signs for 17 years.

Lisa began her career as a teacher in several small towns in Northeastern Minnesota.

Lisa is uniquely qualified to write these devotionals because she and her husband have faced the challenge of owning and operating a small business, being childless, being on the edge of bankruptcy and foreclosure, and living in separate locations for 18 months.

In 2014 Lisa and Tom moved to Fargo, ND, where Lisa began a new job, leaving the sign ministry behind, but not her desire to write. Lisa has led several Women's Bible studies, including The Amazing Collection, all 66 books of the Bible, published by Big Dream Ministries. Lisa is involved with her local church and community. She enjoys knitting, holding her cat, (sometimes at the same time!) cooking, and reading in her spare time.

Visit Lisa's Website to learn more: www.lisadonelson.com

IF YOU ENJOYED THIS BOOK, WILL YOU CONSIDER SHARING IT WITH OTHERS?

- Mention the book in a blog post or through Facebook, Twitter, or Pinterest.
- Recommend this book to those in your small group, book club, workplace, and classes.
- Pick up a copy for someone you know who would be challenged and encouraged by this message.

www.ingramcontent.com/pod-product-compliance
Lightning Source LLC
Chambersburg PA
CBHW042116100526
44587CB00025B/4074